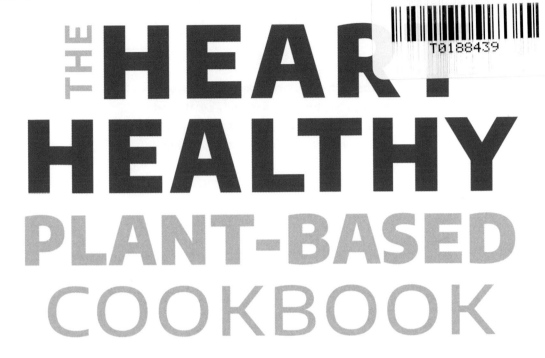

THE HEART HEALTHY
PLANT-BASED COOKBOOK

OVER 100 RECIPES
FOR LOWERING BLOOD PRESSURE, REVERSING HEART DISEASE & CARDIAC RECOVERY

JENNEFFER PULAPAKA, DPM & CHEF HARI PULAPAKA

FOREWORD BY DAVID L. KATZ, MD, MPH

hatherleigh

Hatherleigh Press is committed to preserving
and protecting the natural resources of the earth.
Environmentally responsible and sustainable practices are
embraced within the company's mission statement.

Visit us at www.hatherleighpress.com.

THE HEART HEALTHY PLANT-BASED COOKBOOK

Text copyright © 2024 by Jenneffer Pulapaka, DPM & Hari Pulapaka, PhD

Library of Congress Cataloging-in-Publication Data is available upon request.

ISBN: 978-1-57826-951-8

Cover and Interior Design by Carolyn Kasper

Printed in the United States

10 9 8 7 6 5 4 3 2 1

Contents

Foreword
by David L. Katz, MD, MPH

FAR MORE RECENTLY THAN most now recall—around the middle of the 20th century—the origins of coronary artery disease were unknown. The prevailing view at the time was that cumulative damage to the coronary arteries leading to heart attack, and often death, was an inevitable consequence of aging. Ancel Keys was in the vanguard of those who noted stark population differences in the rate of heart disease and hypothesized that variations in lifestyle (and especially diet) might be implicated. The signature contributions to science and public health of the famous Seven Countries Study had nothing to do with overall dietary fat intake, and only a little to do with saturated fat. Fundamentally, the study demonstrated that heart disease was diet and lifestyle-related, and thus that it could be prevented.

In some ways, how far we have come since the seminal contributions of Keys is quite amazing. Science has established incontrovertibly that diet and lifestyle are overwhelmingly responsible for coronary artery disease, even when genes influencing risks are taken fully into account. There is widespread recognition that at least 80 percent of heart disease in the world could be prevented outright with optimal diet, routine physical activity, and the avoidance of toxins like tobacco. With attention to the full expanse of lifestyle behaviors influencing health—diet, activity, toxic exposures, sleep, stress/mental health/happiness, and social connections/love—the case is strong that heart disease due to atherosclerosis (the accumulation of plaque) can be all but eradicated.

Nor has progress stopped with prevention: studies have shown reductions of up to 80 percent in the rate of recurrent heart attacks and premature death among those with symptomatic heart disease by means of diet and lifestyle as medicine. High-quality dietary patterns, with a primary emphasis on whole plant foods, can not only help stop the progression of atherosclerotic plaque, but actually induce its regression, reversing the process at the foundations of heart disease.

Studies, now routinely gathered under the "food as medicine" rubric, have shown that getting diet right can treat high blood pressure as or more effectively than the best of pharmacotherapy (drugs); do the same for type 2 diabetes; and lower elevated blood lipids as effectively as statin drugs.

In other ways, however, our progress in the past 80 or so years has been painfully scant. Heart disease remains the leading killer of both men and women in this country, and the leading overall cause of premature death. Poor diet quality, a key contributor to that toll, is responsible for more than 500,000 premature deaths annually—year in, year out. Our knowledge has advanced; yet our power to use that knowledge for the good it could do lags far behind.

Why? There are no doubt many reasons, but we might start with this: food is, indeed, medicine. In fact, for cardiometabolic diseases it is the very *best* of medicine. But it is, of course, so much more. Unlike medicine, food is an integral part of our daily routines and most vivid memories; of our comfort and celebrations; of solace, and solidarity. For most of us, food is an important source of pleasure, an indelible daily element in nothing less than our quality of life.

That matters. What, after all, is health for? The intrinsic value of health is what it can purchase: more years in life, more life in years. Other things being equal, healthy people have more fun.

Health and pleasure both matter because none of us simply wants to be alive—we also want to live!

This book, *Heart Healthy Plant-Based Cookbook*, is all about that confluence. Of the various dietary patterns shown to reduce risk for heart attack and improve cardiovascular health, none is quite so storied as a whole-food, plant-exclusive dietary pattern free of added oils. That particular approach, however, imposes restrictions that might seem to put the pleasure of food out of reach, especially for the uninitiated.

Not so. We all owe a debt of gratitude to the team of Hari and Jenneffer Pulapaka—a celebrated chef and a lifestyle medicine practitioner, respectively—for taking on the challenge of making the rarefied, therapeutic potency of a plant-exclusive, no added oil diet respond equally to the imperative of pleasure. Drawing inspiration from cuisines around the world, this book asserts that not only is food the best of medicine for heart disease, but that there should be no hesitation in getting that "medicine" to go down. It can and should be a source of daily delight. The authors rightly extend their recipe of empowerment and hope to span the full range of lifestyle practices that matter in their own right, and influence our interactions with food as well—from sleep, to stress, to social interactions.

Admittedly, if you are accustomed to the standard American diet, the focus here will be a significant change for you. But as part of the intended audience for this book—someone with, or at high risk for, heart disease personally and/or in a loved one—you have good reason to make a significant change. Expert guidance and delicious dishes will ease that journey, and your own taste buds will help. Familiarity is a major determinant of our dietary preferences, and as you get used to a new (and far healthier) way of eating, you will quickly come to prefer it.

However heart disease has intruded into your life and upset it, you no doubt want—and *deserve*—to get your life back. You probably want, and also deserve, more than just having your life back: you also want to live it, fully. Food is an important part of that.

Can you benefit from the transformative power of food as medicine, and still find delight in eating every day? Yes, you can...with the right guidance. *Heart Healthy Plant-Based Cookbook* is the source of just such expert guidance to a place where you can savor delicious food, and celebrate the delights of your health, restored.

— **David L. Katz, MD, MPH**
  Past President, American College of Lifestyle Medicine

Publisher's Note

HEART DISEASE IS THE LEADING cause of death in the United States. According to the Centers for Disease Control (CDC), one person dies every 36 seconds in the United States from cardiovascular disease. One in four deaths can be attributed to heart disease. Coronary artery disease is the most common type of heart disease. In the United States, someone has a heart attack every 40 seconds. High blood pressure, high blood cholesterol, and smoking are key risk factors for heart disease. Several other medical conditions and lifestyle choices can also put people at high risk for heart disease. Diabetes, overweight and obesity, unhealthy diets, physical inactivity, and excessive alcohol use are all significant contributors to heart disease.

This book is an invaluable resource for anyone who has had a heart attack, heart surgery, or who has had a diagnosis or family history of high blood pressure, high cholesterol, and cardiovascular disease. They say that we are what we eat. While this may be true, it is equally true that with our fast-paced lives and access to a wide variety of convenience food, it is increasingly challenging to eat foods that are both tasty and good for you. Evidence-based medical research unequivocally recommends that individuals with cardiac challenges should maintain a whole-food, plant-based diet devoid of excessive sodium or free fats.

Cardiac rehabilitation includes a regimen and lifestyle with adequate physical activity, healthy eating, and reduced stress. We must eat every day, usually multiple times a day. So, becoming educated about a diet which is not only heart healthy and heart strengthening but also enjoyable and satisfying is critical in achieving and maintaining cardiac recovery. Anyone who has a heart problem, or the potential for one, can benefit from cardiac rehabilitation.

In this book, an award-winning professional chef and pioneering lifestyle medicine-certified podiatric surgeon team up to help cardiac at-risk or recovering individuals gently and accessibly navigate diet and lifestyle adjustments towards a healthy and joyful life. This book will prove to you that with a few sustainable changes, a heart-healthy, whole-food, plant-based diet is easy to maintain and can be extremely delicious and satisfying. All the recipes in the book are intentionally no-sodium-added and no-free-fats-added.

—Andrew Flach, Publisher

Who Will Benefit From This Book?

O N SATURDAY, DEC. 10TH, 2011, my step-brother died at age 57 from a massive heart attack/failure while working outside with my nephew. Johnie had a recent physical exam, which he passed without complications. He would exercise on and off and was only slightly overweight. I never heard him mention food or wine restrictions when we would eat over at their house or during a family outing. He and his family were completely unaware of any cardiac issues. In hindsight, we know that cardiac disease is the number one leading preventable cause of death in the United States. This was a journey that would take me 10 years to ascertain the answers to.

Five years after his death, I visited New Orleans for a cooking event and had the opportunity to deviate off the agenda to evaluate the new and upcoming Goldring Center for Culinary Medicine at Tulane University, which was founded in 2012. From then on, I dedicated myself to improving my family and patients through the art of cooking and the science of medicine. I had spent almost a decade in a restaurant that developed local and sustainable flavors that were beyond a decadent experience, and now, I would dedicate my remaining career in medicine to be in collaboration alongside my husband, Hari Pulapaka, to provide healthful dietary options and inspirations. Because the strength of his creations and the complexity of his flavors make it possible to showcase the power and beauty of food as medicine.

This book will help to provide guidance in the future, through the use of a whole food plant-based diet. Additionally, it incorporates key evidence and basic information on a healthy lifestyle, exercise, sleep, and connectivity, which are associated with a lower risk of mortality and cardiovascular disease. If you want to live a heart healthy lifestyle, had a heart attack, have heart disease, or peripheral vascular disease, you can find guidance for your journey with this book. Knowing the hard facts, that one person dies every 36 seconds in the United States from a heart attack or one in four deaths can be attributed to heart disease; sets the stage for why we need proper nutrition to mitigate the impact of cardiovascular disease on our family, friends, and patients.

The Pillars of a Heart Healthy Lifestyle

S O, YOU HAVE BEEN told by your doctor you are at risk for cardiovascular disease and you need to make changes in your life. Perhaps you have been diagnosed with high blood pressure, or are recovering from a heart attack or heart surgery. Whatever the reason, you now find yourself needing to address your fundamental health choices and behaviors and adopt a new framework—a heart healthy lifestyle.

The American College of Lifestyle Medicine recommends the following six pillars as effective strategies for the prevention and treatment of lifestyle-related chronic disease, such as heart disease:

1. **Whole Food, Plant-Based Nutrition.** A diet rich in fiber, antioxidants, and nutrients, focusing on a variety of minimally processed vegetables, fruits, whole grains, legumes, nuts, and seeds.

2. **Physical Activity.** Regular and consistent exercise to combat the negative effects of sedentary behavior.

3. **Restorative Sleep.** Aiming for seven or more hours of sleep per night to support overall health, as sleep disruptions can lead to various health issues.

4. **Stress Management.** Adopting coping mechanisms and reduction techniques to manage stress and improve well-being.

5. **Avoidance of Risky Substances.** Staying away from tobacco and excessive alcohol consumption to reduce the risk of chronic diseases.

6. **Positive Social Connections.** Leveraging relationships and social networks to reinforce healthy behaviors and affect physical, mental, and emotional health.

Eating more fruits and vegetables, performing regular physical activity, avoiding harmful use of tobacco and alcohol, and reducing your salt intake have all been shown to reduce the risk of cardiovascular disease. There are also a number of underlying social determinants of health that apply to CVDs, there are social, economic, and cultural changes, also including poverty, stress, and a few hereditary factors.

Let's take a closer look at each of these pillars.

WHOLE FOOD, PLANT-BASED NUTRITION

What we eat—and how we prepare it—has an incredible impact on our health and well-being. For example, high-calorie foods cooked at high temperatures (known as Advanced Glycation End products, or AGEs) contribute to inflammation in the body and long-term cellular damage, both of which are especially harmful to those at risk for or recovering from cardiovascular difficulties. These AGEs diminish the body's immune response, accelerate vascular damage to tissues, and contribute to impaired fibroblast activity, all of which are important factors in maintaining vascular wall function and perfusion.

On the opposite end of the spectrum, enriching one's diet with antioxidants can decrease inflammation. **Flavonoids** are powerful antioxidants with anti-inflammatory effects, most commonly consumed through food such as citrus fruits, berries, apples, grapes, peppers, onions, broccoli, and other herbs. A whole food, plant-based diet (WFPB) maximizes the antioxidant potential within our cells by focusing on those foods (like green vegetables and berries) which contain the highest number of antioxidants possible.

Inflammation and Heart Health

Heart issues, like heart failure and heart disease, often boil down to inflammation and problems with the cells lining your blood vessels. Eating a lot of fatty foods and processed meats can ramp up inflammation, which can be measured by markers like C-reactive protein (CRP), interleukin-6, and homocysteine. On the bright side, switching to a low-fat, high-fiber, whole-food, plant-based diet can cut these markers by a third in just three weeks. This diet change isn't just good for your heart—it can also reduce pain and tenderness in your joints.

High cholesterol levels also contribute to inflammation and hurt blood vessels, making it easier for clots and plaques to form. People with heart disease and inflammation can see improvements by following a cholesterol-lowering diet. The "Statin Diet," created by Dr. David J.A. Jenkins, can be used to reduce cholesterol levels by including key foods like plant sterols, nuts, soy proteins, and viscous fiber found in beans, eggplant, and oats.

Omega oils also play a role in inflammation. Some, like those found in safflower and sunflower oils, can increase inflammation. But others, like omega-3 fatty acids found in leafy greens, flaxseeds, and walnuts, have the opposite effect. Combining omega-3s with a portfolio diet can lower the risk of heart problems better than relying on medication alone.

Obesity is another player in inflammation. It's linked to proteins like leptin, which connect weight gain to inflammation. When obesity pairs with conditions like high blood pressure and diabetes, it's known as metabolic syndrome, which puts extra stress on your body and can lead to heart disease.

For those with heart troubles, the goal is to boost blood flow, reduce inflammation, and improve how the blood vessels function. Some foods can directly help with these goals. For example, pistachios and red wine contain ingredients that help blood vessels work better. Foods like beets also help by converting nitrates to nitric oxide, which improves blood pressure and vessel health. On the flip side, using antimicrobial mouthwash might reduce nitric oxide production and slightly raise blood pressure.

PHYSICAL ACTIVITY

Physical inactivity is the biggest public health problem of the 21st century, with most individuals only staying active through the normal routines of their daily life. But that's just it—**activities of daily living (ADLs) are not exercise.**

Simply improving aerobic fitness through regular physical activity has the greatest impact on longevity. If worldwide inactivity could be decreased by even 25 percent, more than 1.3 million deaths worldwide could be averted every year.

The U.S. national physical activity guidelines suggest 150 minutes of moderate-intensity exercise per week and 2+ days per week of strength training. Moderate intensity exercises means getting you moving fast enough or strenuously enough to burn off three to six times as much energy per minute as you do when you are sitting quietly. Examples are brisk walking, water aerobics, riding a bike, dancing, and hiking.

RESTORATIVE SLEEP

Your body's critical healing time is during the precious minutes of deep sleep. This is when your body is ready to work hard and recover from the damages of the day. During deep sleep or "slow wave sleep," your body produces its highest levels of growth hormones (GH) and low levels of cortisol, which regulate your body's stress response. GHs fuel your body's cells and help maintain tissues and organs throughout life and cortisol helps to control your body's use of carbohydrates, proteins, and fats. The bottom line is that sleep matters, and as you age, you have to work to get good quality sleep.

Low-quality sleepers are at 45 percent higher risk of myocardial infarction, 140 percent for heart failure, 60 percent for a stroke, and coronary heart disease (CHD) a 30 percent higher risk, as compared to good quality sleepers. **Healthy adults need between seven and nine hours of sleep per night.** Teens and babies require more for their growth and development. People over 65 should also get seven to eight hours of undisturbed sleep per night. With that noted, sleep lasting greater than ten hours or more and afternoon napping, greater than one hour, increases all-cause mortality by 32 percent.

These statistics drive home the point that an excuse of, "I don't have time to sleep," or, "I'm too busy to worry about sleep," can be deadly. Sleep is a powerful tool in your cardiac health, so respect it and use its strength to regenerate and heal your body.

10 Tips for Better Sleep

1. Go to bed and get up at the same time every day, including on the weekends and during vacations.

2. Make sure your bedroom is quiet, dark, relaxing, and at a comfortable temperature.

3. Limit exposure to bright light in the evenings, turn off electronic devices at least 30–60 minutes before bedtime.

4. Establish a relaxing bedtime routine.

5. Exercise! Being physically active during the day can help you fall asleep more easily and sleep more deeply at night.

6. Remove electronic devices, such as TVs, computers, and smartphones, from the bedroom.

7. If you can't fall asleep or wake up and can't get back to sleep after what you think is 20 minutes, get out of bed, read, sketch, or do another calming activity in lowlight.

8. Don't eat a large meal before bedtime. If you are hungry at night, eat a light, healthy snack.

9. Avoid consuming caffeine in the late afternoon or evening. As well, avoid consuming alcohol, nicotine, and THC before bedtime.

10. Reduce your fluid intake before bedtime.

STRESS MANAGEMENT

Psychological distress is common among adults with cardiovascular disease and contributes to a greater risk of cardiovascular events and mortality. Stress management is a way to reduce psychological distress and improve coping among adults with CVD.

Mindfulness-Based Intervention (MBI) is a moment-by-moment awareness of the surrounding environment and personal thoughts, feelings, and bodily sensations. During the practice of mindfulness, there may be a focus on breathing, sitting, walking, or body awareness.

Mindfulness is thought to improve CVD by enhancing an individual's attention control, self-awareness, and emotional self-regulation. **Focused Attention Meditation (FAM),** such as mantras and training awareness, allows individuals to achieve a similar level of awareness found in MBI, but also to focus their attention on an object, sound, or sensation. Chakras meditation is another practice that uses special techniques, such as activation sounds, breathing techniques, and yoga postures.

AVOIDANCE OF RISKY SUBSTANCES

Unhealthy behaviors, such as heavy episodic drinking, smoking, sedentary activity, and poor nutrition, have a monumental impact on one's cardiovascular health. In particular, alcohol abuse can have wide-ranging negative effects, including central nervous system imbalance, dysfunction to the renin-angiotensin system, increased cortisol, impaired cardiac baroreceptors, and increased vasoconstriction by its negative impact on the NO system.

Kicking bad habits like smoking and alcohol and replacing them with healthy routines, like yoga, mindfulness, or exercise through strong networks can lead to a better quality of life and a marked decrease in risk factors for heart attack and stroke.

POSITIVE SOCIAL CONNECTIONS

Spend time with and talk to family and friends, get involved in activities within your community, or reach out to support groups when needed. Find different ways to relax, as mentioned before. Ground down; whether through mindfulness, meditation, yoga, or dance. Remember to take care of your spiritual needs as well.

Positive emotional and behavioral factors may promote cardiovascular health. Recent research suggests that emotion regulation is associated with cardiovascular disease risk, as high as a 20 percent reduced risk of incident coronary heart disease is associated with high levels of self-regulation. These simple techniques involve the ability to manage impulses, feelings, and behaviors. Reach out to your friends or family when you need encouragement. Don't forget to celebrate your success with others. If you have a setback, consider coaching yourself. Don't dwell on things that cannot be changed. Ask the question, "Is there another way to look at the situation?"

Positive emotions like joy, interest, contentment, pride, and love are important emotion regulatory strategies because they both enhance activities (like eating a healthy diet) and mitigate the likelihood of deteriorative behaviors, such as cigarette smoking.

The Key Components of a Whole Food, Plant-Based Diet

WHAT DOES A WHOLE food plant-based (WFPB) diet consist of? It's all about what you can eat first, not what you can't eat. A WFPB diet derives most of its caloric energy from whole, unprocessed, or minimally processed carbohydrates, proteins, and some fats.

The WFPB diet does not include highly processed or refined foods, such as free oils (EVOO, vegetable oils), sugars, bleached flours, and stripped grains. The key is to focus on high-fiber, filling foods that are naturally rich in vitamins and minerals, have low glycemic indices, and relatively low in protein content and caloric density. For a cardiovascular healthy diet, keep the ratios of 15% to 20% monounsaturated fat; 5% to 10% polyunsaturated fat; less than 10% saturated fat; 0% trans fat and 0% cholesterol. A common misconception is that the WFPB diet has few protein options, but this is untrue. New sources of proteins should be explored, including whole grains, seeds, nuts, legumes, peas, and vegetables; different preparations of soy, a variety of lentils, legumes and grains combos, and seaweed preparations.

The list on the next page outlines the types of foods most commonly consumed as part of the daily WFPB diet:

SERVINGS	WHOLE FOOD, PLANT-BASED DIET ITEMS
2	Berries
4	Other fruits
3	Dark greens or cruciferous vegetables
3	Whole grains
3	Beans
1	Flaxseed or chia seeds
1	Nuts
1	Herbs
1	Spices
5	Water

When you fill up on your daily serving, it leaves little room to consume other foods that are less nutrient dense.

When considering starting a whole food plant-based diet, it is essential that you consider how best to incorporate the various macro- and micronutrients your body requires, while still adhering to the restrictions of a WFPB diet.

PROTEIN

Dry beans and lentils (such as soybeans, garbanzo beans, navy beans, kidney beans, pinto beans, Great Northern beans, and black-eyed peas) are excellent sources of protein and can easily take the place of meat and fish. Some other sources of protein found in a plant-based diet are tofu, tempeh, whole grain breads, nuts, and potatoes.

FIBER

Fiber is a component in plants that your body is unable to digest or absorb. There are two main types of fiber—soluble (also called "viscous") and insoluble. While both have health benefits, our focus is on the former, as only soluble fiber reduces the risk of heart disease.

A wealth of research suggests that fiber helps to reduce LDL (bad) cholesterol levels, thereby lowering your risk of heart disease. It also seems to relieve constipation and decrease the symptoms of both diverticulosis and irritable bowel syndrome. High fiber diets even seem to help control blood sugar. This is especially important if you have diabetes or are at risk of developing the disease.

So how does fiber affect your body? Once it enters the digestive tract, soluble fiber mixes with liquid and binds to fatty substances, thus removing it from the body. Once fat has been removed from the body, there is naturally less fat available to make cholesterol. Soluble fiber also prolongs the time it takes for the stomach to empty, meaning sugar is released and absorbed more slowly. This helps to control blood sugar levels.

Ideally, total fiber intake should be about 25 to 30 grams daily with a minimum of 5 to 10 grams coming from soluble fiber. Many foods contain both soluble and insoluble fiber. Generally, fruits have more soluble fiber and vegetables are richer in insoluble fiber.

Good Food Sources of Soluble Fiber

Whole grain cereals and seeds like barley, oatmeal, oat bran, whole-wheat products such as psyllium seeds, (ground) wheat oat, corn bran, flax seed.

Fruits like apples (with the skin), bananas, pears, blackberries, oranges, grapefruits, nectarines, peaches, pears, plums, prunes.

Legumes like black beans, kidney beans, lima beans, navy beans, northern beans, yellow beans, green beans and pinto beans, yellow, green, and orange lentils, chickpeas and black-eyed peas.

Vegetables like broccoli, Brussels sprouts, carrots, green beans, cauliflower, potatoes (with their skin).

IRON

Foods that are rich in iron include soy-based foods, dried fruits, dried beans, spinach, chard, fortified cereals, eggs, legumes, baked potatoes, mushrooms, nuts, beans, tofu, tempeh, and bulgur.

CALCIUM

Calcium is plentiful in low-fat milk, yogurt, and cheese. Other sources include legumes, broccoli, chard, almonds, collard greens, kale, almonds, fortified orange juice, soy milk, and other soy products.

ZINC

Those following a WFPB diet can get their necessary zinc from foods such as nuts, soy beans, soy milk, mushrooms, peas, breads, fortified cereals, wheat germ, and pumpkin seeds.

FAT

Fat benefits our bodies in various ways. It is an energy source for our body; without it, certain vitamins, including A, D, E, and K, could not be absorbed. Furthermore, when fat is converted into fatty tissue, it acts as an insulator, keeping our bodies warm.

The truth is, there are several different types of fat. Knowing which ones raise LDL (bad) blood cholesterol is the first step in lowering your risk of heart disease. Dietary cholesterol, saturated fat, and trans-fats all raise bad blood cholesterol levels. Polyunsaturated and monounsaturated fats do not.

Thankfully, cholesterol is only found in foods of animal origin, meaning a whole food, plant-based diet helps us avoid almost all sources of harmful fats.

Polyunsaturated fat, meanwhile, is most prevalent in plant-based foods. While excluding added oils from one's diet does preclude the more common sources of plant-based polyunsaturated fats, there are still many kinds of nuts that can be used to supplement. A type of polyunsaturated fat, called an omega-3 fatty acid, is currently being studied to see if it helps guard against heart disease.

Omega-3 Fatty Acids

For those who don't eat fish, reliable sources of omega-3 fatty acids are walnuts, soy products, and flaxseed. Some may also choose to take a supplement to make sure they are getting adequate amounts of omega-3 fatty acids.

B-VITAMINS

All vitamins play an important role in keeping our bodies running smoothly, especially the B-complex vitamins. These eight vitamins help break down the carbohydrates, proteins, and fats from your diet into energy.

The three most important B-vitamins for heart health include vitamin B-9 (folic acid), vitamin B6, and vitamin B12. If you get too little folic acid, an amino acid called homocysteine can accumulate in your blood. Homocysteine can potentially harm cells that line the heart and blood vessels. Folic acid works with B6 and B12 to metabolize homocysteine and bring blood levels down to a safe range. If these vitamins are in short supply, homocysteine levels can build up, causing plaque formation around the arteries that can eventually lead to a heart attack.

B-vitamins are water soluble, which means they are easily broken down and absorbed by the body. It also means that you need an ongoing supply, because the kidneys excrete most of what your body doesn't immediately use.

Vitamin B-9 / Folic Acid

Vitamin B-9 is important in red blood cell formation, protein metabolism, growth and cell division. It's also important during pregnancy for the developing fetus. Heart-healthy food sources include citrus fruits, dark leafy greens, nuts, beans, and fortified grain products. Other good sources include cantaloupe, raspberries, oranges, spinach, broccoli, and leaf lettuce. A sure way to get your daily needs of folic acid is to take a multivitamin, but foods offer the benefit of delicious flavor and supply a variety of nutrients.

Vitamin B-6

Vitamin B-6 is essential for protein metabolism, energy production, and brain function. It aids in the formation of several hormones, such as serotonin which regulates sleep and mood. Heart-healthy food sources include skinless chicken, salmon, swordfish, pork loin, soybeans, oats, whole grain products, nuts, seeds, bananas, egg substitutes, and avocados.

Vitamin B12

Vitamin B-12 plays an essential role in red blood cell formation, cell metabolism, and nerve function. An adequate supply is needed to support proper digestion and produce energy from fat and sugar.

On the next page, you'll find more information on common plant-based sources for essential vitamins and nutrients. While this list is by no means exhaustive, it offers a starting point for transitioning to a WFPD while still providing your body with everything it needs to flourish.

Plant-Based Sources of Essential Vitamins

Vitamin A

- Fruits
- Green leafy vegetables
- Yellow vegetables

Vitamin B

- Nuts
- Legumes
- Whole grains
- Green vegetables

Vitamin C

- Green vegetables
- Papayas
- Citrus
- Berries
- Tomatoes

Vitamin D

- Sunlight
- Fortified orange juices
- Some yogurts

Vitamin E

- Whole grains
- Nuts
- Dark green leafy vegetables
- Avocados
- Wheat germ

Meal Planning & Prep Tips

EVEN FOR PROFESSIONAL COOKS, cooking is fun and inspiring only if we are adequately prepared and have undergone the process of planning and organization. In a restaurant, no matter the menu or style of cuisine and operation, it is someone's responsibility to determine inventory and shopping lists on a daily basis. Station cooks are in charge of the shopping and prep needs of their stations. Naturally, the same is true (and possibly to an even greater degree) when cooking at home. Because even though one doesn't cook the volume or diversity of food at home, the home cook is expected to do everything on top of navigating the challenges of daily living.

This chapter is designed to help you multi-task and think ahead when planning and preparing your meals.

Gaining Confidence

First, cook your way through the Level 1 recipes in the book. These are easy recipes with few steps. They could become your routine, go-to recipes that cover a wide range of flavors and possibilities.

Next, identify the two spice blends included in this book which you find interesting and compatible with your palate. Learn to make them (they're all easy, trust me) and always have them on hand, stored at room temperature, in an air-tight container. When you cook dishes that require other spice blends, the task of making one freshly won't seem as unfamiliar or tedious.

Repeat Step 2 above for the chutneys and sauces included in this book but be sure to keep them refrigerated. Use them up before making new ones or new batches.

SHOPPING & STORAGE TIPS

Consider dedicating a specific day and time period of the week for grocery shopping. Try to avoid known busy times in your chosen grocery store, but that may not always be possible.

Ensure that your refrigerator and pantry are ready to accept new additions.

Select the recipes and meals you want to cook for a significant portion of the week. Prepare a shopping list. This keeps your pantry stocked as well as helping to mitigate impulse shopping.

Prior to shopping, check your pantry and refrigerator. Often, ingredients in recipes can be substituted with others you may already have (see page 27 for herb and spice substitutions). In that case, especially if what you have is perishable, go with the substitution and account for that in your shopping list.

Practice first in, first out (FIFO) with the storage of perishable ingredients like vegetables, herbs, and non-dairy milks. Be mindful of how long perishables have been in the refrigerator. Take advantage of customized temperature sections of your refrigerator to optimize storage conditions for ingredients.

Portion your meals and refrigerate leftover portions in airtight labeled containers.

If you don't anticipate using items within the next few days or find yourself away from home for an extended period of time, freeze them after labeling.

The next chapter provides a comprehensive and aspirational list of kitchen tools and items to stock your pantry with. Try to keep your pantry stocked at least 50%. This will ensure the ability to cook quick weekday meals without having to dash to the grocery store each time.

PREP SUGGESTIONS

✓ **Pick a prep day, perhaps on the weekend.** Allow it to be fun. Perhaps team up with a partner, friend, or family member.

✓ **Always be mindful of how long steps take** and how long a dish takes from preparation to completion. With repetition, you will notice how much more proficient and efficient everything becomes. Expect some inertia when you first start, but that is a normal aspect of any new activity. Don't be discouraged.

✓ **Don't be hesitant to make larger quantities,** especially of the soups. Leftovers when stored properly and immediately can be wonderful a day or two later. Many dishes in this book are designed to taste even better the next day or after.

✓ **If you choose to cook beans from a** dried stage (see page 202), be sure to always have a batch of cooked beans dressed in a bit of apple cider vinegar in the refrigerator. This would be a prep day type of activity.

✓ **Design theme nights.** We know about "Meatless Mondays" and "Taco Tuesdays," but it's more fun to invent your own. For example, *Sandwich Saturdays*, *Soup Sundays*, *Mediterranean Mondays*, *Turmeric Tuesdays*, *Waste Not Wednesdays*, *Tofu Thursdays*, *Fancy Fridays*, you get the idea. Have fun, stay inspired, and most importantly, make these ideas your own.

✓ **Clean and organize as you go!**

Kitchen Tools, Essential Pantry & Plant-Based Alternatives

A STREAMLINED PANTRY STOCKED WITH essential flavorful and nutritional ingredients goes a long way in facilitating creative, scratch-cooking at home. Furthermore, the hand-picked ingredients will allow for tailor-made and satisfying flavor in every meal. Here are recommended pantry ingredients that will help make cooking delicious, heart-healthy, whole food, plant-based meals at home enjoyable and easy. In general, avoid highly processed ingredients. However, to truly achieve a diverse 100% whole food diet, one must go to great lengths, have substantial time and culinary expertise.

Having appropriate kitchen tools makes the activity of cooking both enjoyable and efficient. The list below is aspirational, so if you cannot obtain all of them, prioritize the list as needed.

Useful Kitchen Tools

- Baking Sheet Trays
- Bowls
- Can O pener
- Cast-Iron Skillet
- Chef Knife
- Coffee Grinder (for spices)
- Colander or Strainer
- Cutting Board
- Dry Ingredient Measuring Cups
- Fine Strainer
- Food Processor
- Heat-resistant Spatula
- High Performance Blender
- Knife Steel and Sharpener
- Liquid Ingredient Measuring Cups
- Measuring Spoons
- Microplane (or Zester)
- Non-Stick Pan
- Paring Knife
- Pot (with lid)
- Saucepan (with lid)
- Sauté pans
- Serrated Knife
- Silicone Non-Stick Baking Liner (like Silpat®)
- Stock Pot (with lid)
- Tongs
- Weighing Scale
- Whisk
- Wooden Spoon

Take the simple example of bread or pasta. Unless one grinds their own flour from a whole grain, anything store-bought would involve a level of processing. So, the goal is to maximize the percentage of whole foods in your diet while minimizing the percentage of store-bought processed ingredients.

- **Beans (canned, no-sodium):** broad beans, small red beans, kidney beans, black beans, garbanzo (chickpeas), pinto beans, cannellini beans, navy beans
- **Cooking Wines:** Pinot Grigio, Merlot
- **Flours:** Whole wheat flour, garbanzo flour, teff flour, brown rice flour, whole wheat all-purpose flour
- **Fresh Fruit:** blueberries, blackberries, raspberries, oranges, apples, cantaloupe, papaya, grapes, cranberries, pears, pomegranates, grapefruit
- **Fresh Herbs:** basil, cilantro, chives, green tea leaves, parsley, tarragon, thyme
- **Grains:** Whole oats, brown rice, barley, bulgur, quinoa, farro
- **Greens:** arugula, spinach, collard greens, mustard greens, kale, swiss chard, beet greens
- **Legumes (dry):** split peas, red lentils, brown lentils, green lentils, mung beans, kidney beans, garbanzo beans
- **Legumes (frozen):** soybeans, black-eyed peas, green peas, lima beans, field peas
- **Milks (nut-based):** soy milk, oat milk, almond milk, corn milk
- **Nuts and Seeds:** peanuts, walnuts, hazelnuts, macadamia nuts, pistachios, almonds, flax seeds, chia seeds, pumpkins seeds, sesame seeds, hemp
- **Other:** Nutritional yeast, vital gluten, nori, wakame
- **Soy Products:** extra-firm tofu, silken tofu
- **Spices:** cayenne, cumin, coriander, fennel, garlic powder, onion powder, paprika, sumac, turmeric, black pepper
- **Sweeteners:** date sugar, date syrup
- **Vegetables:** asparagus, broccoli, Brussels sprouts, carrots, red bell peppers, tomatoes, acorn squash, sweet potatoes, onions, garlic, ginger
- **Vinegars:** dark balsamic, white balsamic, red wine, apple cider, rice wine, sherry

EGG ALTERNATIVES
Aquafaba

Aquafaba is the left-over liquid obtained after cooking legumes like chickpeas. A preserved version is the gelatinous liquid found in canned legumes. When possible, re-hydrate dried legumes and cook them yourself for a more unadulterated version. To use aquafaba to make, say, a vegan alternative for traditional mayonnaise, simply season with lemon juice and a small amount of coconut cream before blending with a high-speed hand blender for about 10 minutes.

Flaxseed (aka Linseed)

An antioxidant-packed seed, flaxseed is useful in baking as a binder. Simply mix ground flaxseed with three times the volume of water and let the mixture sit for 10 minutes.

Chia Seed

Chia seed is similar to flaxseed. Either the seed itself or a ground version can be used. Typically, a 2.5-part water to 1-part chia seems to do a consistent job. Again, allow the mixture to sit for 10 minutes before using as a binder.

Tapioca Starch Slurry

Tapioca starch is a consistent gluten-free flour, and when mixed with water to make a paste or slurry, it may be used as a thickener for sauces, fillings, and even for baking. Its neutral flavor and color make it a versatile thickener.

Garbanzo Flour or Paste

Just like tapioca starch, garbanzo (chickpea) flour offers a way to thicken sauces without using dairy or eggs. Simply mix with an equal amount of water to make a paste. There is no need to let the paste rest. One must also be aware of the inherent nutty flavor of chickpeas.

DAIRY ALTERNATIVES
Nut-Based

There has been quite the uproar and push back from the dairy industry regarding the use of the word "milk" for any product not derived from animals. Nevertheless, there is no denying the impact of coconut milk and soy milk, specifically, and to a lesser degree, almond milk, or cashew milk, as a non-dairy option. From a cooking point of view, coconut milk is the most versatile and, frankly, delicious. However, coconut milk tends to be higher in saturated fats, which explains its decadent mouthfeel. None of the nut-based milks are particularly stable under the duress of high heat or long cooking times required in certain dishes. Nut-based dairy alternatives are most effective when used to finish cooked sauces or dishes. Additionally, their flavor is distinctive, and one needs to account for that in any given dish.

Grain-Based

Oat milk is delicious and extremely versatile. Its higher fat content translates as a good approximation to traditional dairy. Its flavor is extremely conducive to cooking. Other types of grain-based dairy substitutes are derived from rice and even quinoa. In this book, many recipes call for oat milk.

Soy milk is very popular and easily available. Sometimes, it's best if tofu doesn't quite taste like tofu. There is no mistaking the distinctive flavor of tofu. Young soybeans, on the other hand, have a different flavor profile. Blended silken tofu mixed with a bit of water is thick and may be used in place of heavy cream. The flavor is another matter. Functionally, it works well. Commercial soymilk is available in a variety of flavors and sweetness levels.

What about **cheese substitutes?** Every so often, you may have the urge to treat yourself to a homemade, healthy pizza. What does one do for cheese? There are many plant-based cheese substitutes available in the grocery store, but they can be very heavy on fats and sodium. It is very easy to make reasonable alternatives to cheeses without the guilt of breaking your diet. See pages 199– 201 for home recipes.

PLANT-BASED PROTEINS
Tofu

Tofu is a food made from the curds of soybean milk. It is very nutritious and is rich in protein, iron and omega-3 fats. It also contains high amounts of selenium, a mineral needed for the antioxidant system to work properly. Tofu is a popular choice because in addition to being wholesome, it takes on the flavor of the other ingredients in the dish and is extremely versatile.

Tofu is sold in a variety of textures ranging from silken to extra-firm. Depending on the application, choosing the appropriate texture is just as important as marinating the tofu before using. Despite what some would recommend, tofu is somewhat resistant to taking on other flavors. The trick is to puncture the tofu with a fork and then rub on a wet marinade before marinating for many hours, preferably overnight.

Alternately, dry roasting firm or extra-firm tofu shreds in the oven at 325°F for about an hour will dehydrate it to a texture reminiscent of tofu crumbles without any of the factory processing.

Soy nuggets

Soy nuggets are very common in many South Asian countries. My mother used to rehydrate soy nuggets in warm water for 30 minutes before squeezing out the extra water. We found it interesting and tasty when used in bhajis or curries. My mother did this purely as a nutritional supplement. Lately, I have re-discovered this product which is widely available in Indian grocery stores.

Tempeh

Tempeh is a fermented, soy-based product. Its texture is already interesting, and it marinates well, so it grills and pan-roasts really well. Its naturally nutty flavor offers richness and decadence. However, store bought tempeh does contain salt, so avoid it except in moderation or as a bulker in larger volumes.

Seitan

Seitan is wheat gluten that is cooked in a broth of soy sauce, ginger, garlic, or seaweed. Wheat gluten is the essential protein found in wheat. Think of it as a chewy and spongy bread. Its flavor is rather neutral and, consequently, makes for a versatile alternative to mild flavored meats like chicken. Seitan provides an interesting and satisfying form and spongy meat-like texture along with significant dietary protein. (Seitan is not suitable for those on a gluten-free diet.)

Ingredient Substitutions: Quick Reference

Meat: Substitute tofu, tempeh, beans, or cheese to make them meatless.

Meat, poultry, or seafood stocks: Replace them with vegetable stock, vegetable bouillon cubes, miso (which is fermented soybean paste) that is diluted with water, or the water leftover after cooking vegetables, pasta, or beans.

Cheese: The cheese in many recipes can be replaced with tofu, or soy or nut-based cheeses.

Milk: Soy milk, rice milk, or nut milk will serve as acceptable substitutes in recipes that call for dairy-based milk.

Eggs: To replace eggs in your recipes—especially baked goods—try using other binding agents such as mashed banana (1 small banana per egg) or applesauce. When cooking vegetarian burgers or loaves, you can substitute mashed potatoes, tomato paste, moistened breadcrumbs, or rolled oats. An ounce of mashed tofu per egg will work well as a substitute in many breakfast dishes.

COMMON SPICE SUBSTITUTIONS

INGREDIENT	SUBSTITUTION	INGREDIENT	SUBSTITUTION
Ajwain	Dried thyme	Kaffir lime	Lime/lemon
Allspice	Cinnamon/cloves/nutmeg	Kokam	Tamarind/lemon/lime
Anise	Dried fennel	Lavender	Tarragon
Arrowroot	Tapioca/potato starch	Lemon balm	Lemon zest
Asafoetida	Garlic/onion powder	Lemon grass	Lemon/lime zest
Basil	Oregano	Lemon thyme	Lemon/thyme
Bay	Thyme	Lemon verbena	Lemon grass/lemon zest
Borage	Bay leaves/nasturtium	Loomi	Dried lime/lime zest
Caraway	Cumin/dill	Lovage	Celery/parsley/chervil
Cardamom	Nutmeg/cinnamon	Mace	Nutmeg
Cayenne	Any spicy pepper	Marjoram	Oregano
Chervil	Fennel	Mint	Parsley/basil/shiso
Chinese five spice	See recipe	Mustard	Wasabi
Chinese parsley	Celery leaves	Nasturtium	Watercress/arugula
Chives	Onion/garlic	Nutmeg	Mace/cinnamon
Cilantro	Parsley/mint	Oregano	Basil
Cinnamon	Nutmeg/allspice	Paprika	Cayenne (much less)
Clove	Allspice	Parsley	Celery tops/cilantro
Coriander	Cumin	Pink peppercorns	Green peppercorns
Cilantro	Cilantro/cumin	Rosemary	Sage/thyme
Cumin	Coriander	Saffron	Turmeric/paprika
Curly parsley	Cilantro	Sage	Rosemary
Curry leaves	Bay/lime/basil	Savory	Thyme/sage
Curry powder	Turmeric/cumin/coriander	Shiso	Lemon zest/mint
Dill	Tarragon/fennel	Sorrel	Spinach/lemon zest
Epazote	Oregano/savory/cilantro	Star anise	Fennel/allspice
Fennel	Dill	Sumac	Lemon/coriander
Fenugreek	Coriander	Tamarind	Lime/lemon/sugar
Galangal	Ginger	Tarragon	Lavender/dill/fennel
Garlic powder	Onion powder	Thai basil	Basil
Ginger powder	Turmeric/fennel	Thyme	Sage/rosemary
Grains of paradise	Cardamom	Turmeric	Mustard powder
Herbs de Provence	See recipe	Za'tar	Thyme/sesame

Organization, Developing Flavor & Cooking with Spices

PREPARATION & ORGANIZATION

Once you have gathered all your ingredients, visualize, and write down your precooking prep list. If something needs to be oven-roasted, get it going while you continue prepping for other dishes. Even the number of pots and pans on the stove should be a function of only the items that need immediate cooking. Collecting ingredients or utensils before needing them creates unnecessary clutter, which takes up valuable space. A cluttered environment causes avoidable stress in a kitchen.

Another benefit of a list is that it facilitates multi-tasking. As a simple example, if you need onions for both a braised dish and some polenta, prepare enough onions to satisfy both needs. Say that you need a medium to large dice for the braised dish and a mince for the polenta. By doing the onion all at once, you are prepping the same ingredient, using the same knife and cutting board and using one bowl to hold both cuts (separated of course). *Mis en place* constitutes a way of life where every action is enacted—consciously at first, instinctively over time, to save space, prepping time, cleaning time, and increase efficiency. The over-arching benefits are, of course, timely task completion, meaning that one is left with enough time to enjoy the fruits of the labor in the company of your guests over thoughtful food and wine.

I am often asked, "How do you know which flavors to combine?" Frankly, I don't always know. But I have a strong foundation of finding balance in food. That is the key—balance. Balance in no way means that every bite tastes the same or that a spoonful is simply a miniature version of the bowl. Rather, I mean that there are sufficient complementary flavors that highlight each other. Too many flavors can result in a muddled composition. Sometimes, the simplicity of an in-season, perfectly ripe tomato with a pinch of freshly ground black pepper is a magical experience. Some common rules of thumb can help develop powerful flavor combinations from the simple and serene to the complex and intriguing. For example, acidity naturally whets our taste buds to receive more flavor, so many chefs finish their dishes with a squeeze of a fresh lemon or lime.

To develop flavor is to facilitate the transformation of an ingredient with time and proper handling so that it hits peak flavor at the same time it is ready to be consumed. Reduction is the most common technique to help develop and intensify the flavors of sauces and soups. The conventional wisdom is to cover a simmering dish. Well, if the purpose is to simply cook the ingredient, then as long as the cooking liquid is properly seasoned, that technique is valid. Most deep flavors, however, are achieved by cooking things low and slow.

Here are some specific techniques and approaches that will help you achieve deep and satisfying flavors.

Smoking: Barbecue titillates the taste buds because of its deep connections to decadent and rich flavors. Smoking vegetables is underutilized. Season or marinate them overnight and smoke them covered for a while. Finish uncovered. Some vegetables that are great when smoked are tomatoes, peppers, cauliflower, greens, summer squash, winter gourds, cabbage, and onions. Generally, juicy vegetables do well under this preparation, but par-cooking firmer vegetables prior to the barbecue steps yields amazing results. After smoking the vegetables, use them as is or incorporate them into other dishes.

Roasting: Not everyone has a smoker, but almost everyone in North America has an oven. Roasting intensifies the flavor and showcases the natural sugars, providing a tasty snack or satisfying way of incorporating the vegetables into other preparations.

Using Spices: Indian cuisine, better (and more) than any other cuisine, specializes in the use of spices. The reason Indian cuisine is so satisfying for vegetarians worldwide is that the dishes are fraught with deep and savory flavors, thanks to the knowledgeable and experienced use of spices. For the record, spicy doesn't necessarily mean hot (pungent). So, anyone who thinks they don't like spices perhaps just doesn't like the pungency of capsaicin. By layering the flavors of vegetables during the cooking process with a variety of spices, the result can be both nutritious and delicious. Many spices are even known to have a medicinal value, specifically heart health benefits.

Sauces: Vegetables lend themselves to sauce. Instead of simply stir-frying them and accompanying them with a starch or grain, develop a repertoire of sauces that complement the flavor of the prepared vegetable. This book has recipes for many versatile and delicious sauces to make your meals enjoyable and diverse (see pages 203–215).

Seasonality: In most grocery stores in the United States, many vegetables are available year-round, which is unthinkable in many vegetarian-forward countries. Because the consumers demand them, they are supplied. Unfortunately, the cost of omnipresent availability is the flavor. Staging vegetables at various levels of ripeness in temperature-controlled facilities before supplying them to the market has sucked the flavor out of most of them during the off-season. By focusing on seasonal vegetables, one can better enjoy the benefits of their flavor and nutritional value.

NOBODY'S PERFECT

The best chefs in the world make mistakes with food preparation. **But the best chefs also learn from their mistakes.** I learn something new every single day, both in the classroom and in the kitchen. There are very few instances when a mistake in the kitchen cannot be fixed. If something is burnt, make a dip. If something is too acidic, add a non-dairy milk or stir it into a bland starch like rice or potatoes. If something is too spicy (although I don't think that's really a mistake), add some natural sweetness and again, dairy to take the edge off. Almost all food is edible. Except, of course, when unredeemable spoilage occurs.

The recipes in this series progress in the natural way, from breakfast, lunch, dinner, and desserts to accompaniments like spices, chutneys to sauces. These recipes are simply guidelines to prepare a dish. Of course, as chefs, we hope that all our guests enjoy everything we create. But obviously, our taste buds and palates are as different as they are unique.

So, the main purpose of a recipe should be to teach and share the joy of being able to achieve excitement, intrigue, balance, harmony, and satisfaction with ingredients. It should also acknowledge the variability in what we taste and like. The amount of acidity, spice, garlic, and so forth, are subject to interpretation and preference. Yet, by using appropriate and proper cooking techniques and layering soulfully developed flavors, the outcomes serve as useful canvasses for further individualized experimentation and fine-tuning. If a general recipe calls for eggplant, I can tell you from experience that not all eggplant tastes the same. The eggplant in India tastes different from the eggplant in a specific Central Florida farmers' market or grocery store. The soil, water, fertilizer, seed variety, growing cycle, etc. all have some effect on the final flavor.

In that case, why bother with recipes, one might wonder? Well, there is a lot of value in knowing proportions and certainly the chemical reactions significantly affect the outcome. Measurements are more about the relative proportions. In many of the recipes that follow, I try to offer some modifications, in case there is an ingredient you cannot use, are averse to, or simply isn't available.

After making each recipe, try to make every recipe your own by changing the ingredients, seasonings, or proportions to fit your preference after tasting it the way I have prescribed it. Only then can you unlock the full potential of what that dish can mean for you.

COOKING WITH SPICES

Generally, **spices** are aromatics that are used to flavor and season ingredients and sauces. Technically, **a spice can be any part of a plant except the leaves** (which are called herbs). Hence, spices may be derived from stems, roots, flowers, seeds, and bark. The single most important thing to do is to either dry-toast spices to release the essential oils or to bloom them in warm oil (not water).

According to the Oxford English Dictionary, the word spice can be used to refer to "an aromatic or pungent vegetable substance used to flavor food." This is an extremely broad definition; by this measure a vegetable itself could be a spice. But most of us would agree that not all vegetables are spices.

The most common misconception is that spices are spicy. When a dish has a lot of capsaicin, we would refer to it being pungent because of the sensation it stimulates. India may be the land of spices, but that doesn't mean that all Indian cuisine uses spices. For the most part, Indian cuisine is stereotyped in the tourist sections of major Indian cities, as well as outside India with all too familiar dishes. North Indian cuisine has done a masterful job of marketing itself around the globe, and recently, South Indian cuisine (what I grew up with) has made a debut on the world stage.

I suppose the same could be said about the growing understanding that Indian cuisine is diverse and regionally influenced. Spices were historically used for preservation because of the general lack of refrigeration, especially in remote areas. I remember using turmeric on my wounds as an antiseptic. At home, we used numerous whole spices and just a few ground varieties. The word "masala" refers to a spice mix; however, it could also refer to a mix of fresh ingredients to make the base of a sauce or to marinate ingredients. Everyday cooking did not involve the use of excessive spices and was always simple and highlighted the vegetables. In Telugu, the word "kamma" refers to something being savory (not the herb). This is akin to the notion of "umami" and usually involves the use of a minimal number of spices.

It is very important to toast or bloom spices using consistent, low to medium heat in a dry or moist environment. This process releases their essential oils. (The same is true for nuts.) Spices can certainly get stale sitting unused on kitchen shelves for months on end. They lose their aroma and, to some degree, their flavor. Dry toasting them before use helps bring them back to some life. It is still difficult to achieve the fine grind of a store-bought spice because commercial grinders are obviously more powerful. Investing in a high-powered coffee grinder is useful for the sole purpose of grinding freshly toasted spices. In North American cuisine, while it is common to add spices to a simmering soup like a chili, in Indian cuisine the spices or masalas would be added to heated oil or during the sauté stage. This is a fundamental step which must not be omitted.

For beginners, a simple staple blend is one-part ground cumin, one-part ground coriander (the seed of the cilantro plant), half part ground turmeric, and half part ground paprika (or cayenne depending on how pungent one likes it). Curry powder sold in grocery stores is heavy on the turmeric and distinctive in flavor and aroma. Even in India, home cooks do use store bought blends of spices, but the varieties and combinations are targeted at specific dishes rather than a generic "curry" flavor profile.

Whole spices are a great way to infuse the intoxicating aroma and flavor of spices in a dish without the fear of overpowering it. Once again, blooming the spices early in the cooking process is important. The advantage is once the dish is finished, one can remove the whole spices. In classical French cooking, the use of a bouquet garni accomplishes the same result. A bouquet garni consists of aromatics like bay leaves, thyme, peppercorns, and parsley tied into a cheese cloth pouch with a butcher's twine. It fortifies stocks, soups, and sauces.

Upon completion of the dish, the pouch is fished out and discarded. Certainly, one could use a bouquet garni filled with various combinations of whole spices. If whole spices are left in the dish overnight, they have a propensity to intensify the flavor of the dish, but they will also soften, potentially resulting in inadvertently consuming them whole, which might be somewhat unpleasant—although growing up, I used to eat whole cinnamon bark and cloves just for the fun of it.

For the beginner user of spices, I would recommend buying only small quantities. Unfortunately, even small quantities are extremely expensive in grocery stores. For those who grow herbs, drying them is a great way to save money. Just leaving them on a flat sheet in a dry area for a few days will naturally dry them. Doing so on the lowest setting in an oven works as well. For the experienced user of spices, it is a matter of developing a deeper understanding of the interactions between them and how they react to cooking. Ultimately, it is a matter of personal taste. But to truly develop the flavor of a dish which uses spices, using the proper amount of heat, blooming, and resting is important. A dish with spices usually tastes better after it has rested for a bit because the spices have had a chance to harmonize.

THE RECIPES

ABOUT THE RECIPES IN THIS BOOK

Cooking for heart health requires cutting or even eliminating sodium. It also demands a reduction in free fats (oils, dairy, meats, etc.). In this book, every recipe is devoid of added sodium and free fats. We achieve flavor and seasoning in a myriad of other ways including the addition of acidity, the use of spices, and good cooking techniques and flavor combinations. We recommend using more or less acidity based on personal preference.

There are **eight categories** of recipes in this book:

- They say **breakfast** is the most important meal of the day. Anyone can toast bread or scramble some eggs, but the list of breakfast recipes in this book demonstrate the variety, flavor, and nutrition that is possible with just a bit of re-imagination. Most of the breakfast recipes require only a few ingredients and can prepared in only a few steps. Practice makes perfect, so repetition will make them seem trivial after a few times.

- A good **lunch** can set the tone for a fulfilling day. The lunch recipes in this book range from heart healthy salads and soups to familiar yet creative sandwiches and bowls. Also included are light and fast recipes that involve casual picking whether it be at a picnic or at work. Any lunch recipe can be made for dinner and vice-versa.

- The **dinner** recipes showcase the possibilities for preparing whole food, plant-based, heart-healthy meals inspired by familiar dishes world-wide and also some creative options. Any dinner recipe may also be scaled back to a lunch preparation.

- We present five easy-to-make plant-based **desserts** that will round off any meal. They may be used as templates for creating a wide assortment of variations. There are many recipes for plant-based desserts available freely on the Internet, but be sure to read the ingredients carefully, especially for their use of refined sugars and flours.

- The **pantry and pre-cooking** recipes are miscellaneous recipes for items whose functions range from being binders, dairy, and egg substitutes, or providing power-packed plant-based protein in your meals. There are notes about how to use the item. The section also contains directions on how to prepare and cook dried beans.

- **Sauces** form the foundation of all professional cooking. Every cuisine in the world is highlighted by sauces and gravies that bring a distinctness. Naturally, aromatic vegetables, spices, and herbs play an important role in sauce-making. The sauce recipes in this book will give you a wide portfolio of go-to flavors that will help make your food delicious, satisfying, and heart-healthy. With them, you can enjoy a quick weekday meal with very little time and effort.

- The **chutneys and relishes** provide flavorful, internationally-inspired, accompaniments for your meals along with insight into how to bring satisfying balance and brightness to your overall cooking.

- The **spice blends** offer versatile flavor combinations that will elevate the dishes, infuse global flavors, and avoid the sodium and staleness of store-bought spice blends.

All recipes containing beans in this book call for no-sodium canned beans for convenience and to shorten the cooking time. However, by starting with dried beans, one can achieve better flavor, better nutrition, and more control over the seasonings and application. We provide guidelines on cooking dried beans on page 202.

The recipes are presented as follows:

- **Title** of the recipe.

- **Introduction** to the recipe with culinary comments.

- **Degree of difficulty** of the preparation rated on a 1–3 scale, with 1 being the easiest. The Level 1 recipes should be considered a part of one's go-to list of dishes that are made easily and without much fuss. Level 2 recipes are still extremely accessible and will often follow similar steps to Level 1 recipes. Level 2 recipes typically require a few more ingredients and steps. Level 3 recipes are intended for the aspirational cook who wants to go beyond the familiar. After making some Level 2 recipes, Level 3 recipes will be a seamless endeavor and I urge you to try at least one. The recipes in each category are sorted in increasing order of level (Level 1, then Level 2, followed by Level 3).

- **Yield** or number of servings.

- **Heart Health Notes** when applicable highlighting particular ingredients and their known benefits to improving heart health and overall nutrition.

- **Ingredients list.** Please refer to the substitutions table on page 26 if you are missing ingredients.

- A **step-by-step method** of preparation.

> Over 50% of the recipes in this book are at Level 1 based on the steps in the method of preparation. So, while a recipe may call for a few different ingredients, preparing the dish is usually very straightforward.

Breakfast

A NOURISHING START TO THE day will help keep you on the path to a healthy body, mind, and spirit. The recipes in this section are meant to give you familiar options as well as others that break the monotony. With a little bit of preparation and planning, these breakfast options will seem increasingly easy with each rendition.

Heart Healthy Avocado Toast

LEVEL 1   **SERVINGS: 4**

Avocado toast has become a ubiquitous breakfast menu item in restaurants and cafes. This version gives a more interesting option with all the benefits of heart healthy greens and spices.

 HEART HEALTH NOTE: Kale, high in nitrate content, contributes to the production of NO levels. NO, a main vasoactive effector, has antioxidant functions as well. In order to gain the maximum benefits of kale, eat it, *don't* juice it. The NO pathway starts in the mouth with the salivary enzymes which convert nitrate to nitrites and, eventually, NO.

2 cups fresh kale, picked, washed, dried, and chopped

1 tablespoon Bahārāt spice blend (see page 239)

2 lemons, separate the juice and zest

2 cloves fresh garlic, minced

1 small red onion, sliced thinly

8 slices of whole wheat or multigrain bread

4 ripe avocados, smashed

4 medium ripe tomatoes, chopped

1. In a bowl, massage the kale with half the Bahārāt spice blend, half the lemon juice and zest, garlic, and onions. Set aside for 10 minutes.

2. Toast the bread in a toaster or oven on both sides. Allow it to cool.

3. Spread the avocado on the toast. Sprinkle some Bahārāt spice on this layer.

4. Next, place a layer of kale-onion-garlic-lemon mixture evenly on the avocado.

5. Finish with the chopped tomato, some more Bahārāt, and a sprinkle of lemon juice and lemon zest.

Berry & Nut Parfait

LEVEL 1   SERVINGS: 4

This recipe can be made on your prep day, portioned, and refrigerated. However, if you make this well ahead of when you plan to enjoy it, save the addition of the nuts for the last minute.

 HEART HEALTH NOTE: The polyphenols in pomegranates and berries are cardioprotective and increase endothelial cells. Catechins are polyphenols found in pomegranates that are antioxidants and inhibitors of TNF-α, an immune cell signaler. TNF-α is also known to increase ROS levels and decrease nitric oxide production in blood vessels, which can lead to endothelial dysfunction.

8 ounces dairy-free, nonfat yogurt

1 cup blueberries

¼ cup fresh pomegranates

2 fresh peaches, de-seeded and chopped

1 ripe banana, sliced

1 teaspoon aged balsamic vinegar

1 tablespoon date syrup

1 tablespoon walnuts

2 tablespoons pistachios with skin

¼ cup fresh mint, chopped

1. In the bottom of a cup or glass bowl, place ⅓ of a serving of fruit.

2. Next, add a ⅓ of a serving of yogurt.

3. Add a few drops of date syrup and balsamic vinegar.

4. Repeat layers.

5. Sprinkle the top of the parfait with some fresh mint and chopped walnuts and pistachios.

Healthy Breakfast Scramble

LEVEL 1   **SERVINGS: 4**

Breakfast scrambles are typically built on scrambled eggs. Here, the sweet potatoes and mushrooms provide a satisfying umami.

 HEART HEALTH NOTE: Mustard greens are high in nitrates and are a positive contributor to the salivary NO pathway. Additionally, they have significant fiber and antioxidants, Vitamin A and C.

2 whole sweet potatoes, washed and chopped with the skin on

2 cups mustard greens, chopped

2 cups cremini or similar mushrooms, chopped

1-inch piece fresh ginger, peeled and minced

1 large red onion, chopped finely

1 teaspoon ground turmeric

½ teaspoon cayenne (optional)

1 cup apple cider vinegar

2 cups water, more or less

1 teaspoon Dijon Mustard

8 walnut halves, chopped

1. Combine all the ingredients except the walnuts and mustard in a pan.

2. Cook covered on medium until sweet potatoes are soft. This will take about 15 minutes. Uncover and continue cooking until most of the liquid has evaporated.

3. Taste and adjust the acidity. Add a dash more vinegar, if preferred.

4. Finish by mixing in the mustard.

5. Serve with a sprinkle of chopped walnuts.

Greens Smoothie Bowl

LEVEL 1   **SERVINGS: 4**

Having a good blender is priceless for cooking at all levels. The nice thing about this recipe is that it is versatile and quick. Substituting recommended greens with whatever you have on hand is perfectly reasonable.

 HEART HEALTH NOTE: Granny Smith apples are high in flavonoids, decrease circulating triglycerides and help prevent ROS-induced injury.

1 cup fresh kale

1 Granny Smith apple, cored and chopped

1 cup fresh spinach

1 cup fresh watercress

2 ripe avocados, de-seeded

2 cups unsweetened soy milk

1 ripe banana, peeled and sliced

2 lemons, juice and zest

½ cup fresh basil

½ cup fresh strawberries, chopped

¼ cup hazelnuts or macadamia nuts, chopped

1. Blend all the ingredients except the strawberries and nuts to a smooth consistency.

2. Pour into a bowl and garnish with the fresh strawberries and chopped nuts.

Blueberry & Oats Pancakes

LEVEL 1   **SERVINGS: 4**

Pancakes are a popular breakfast item. This recipe is gluten-free barring any cross-contamination that may occur in the oat processing factory. By freezing berries in the height of their season, you can have access to them year-round. These days, grocery stores carry berries year-round, however, they are extremely perishable when purchased outside their season.

 HEART HEALTH NOTE: Oat milk contains the dietary fiber content lacking in cow's milk and can result in significantly lower serum total cholesterol, along with pronounced decreases in LDL cholesterol. Even when oat milk is deprived of insoluble fiber, it still has cholesterol-reducing properties.

1 cup rolled oats

¼ cup oat milk

1 tablespoon baking powder

1 tablespoon apple cider vinegar

½ teaspoon ground nutmeg

1 teaspoon vanilla extract

1 tablespoon date sugar or date syrup

Zest of 1 lemon

1 cup fresh or frozen blueberries

1. Blend all your ingredients, except the blueberries, to a smooth batter. Fold in the blueberries.

2. Let the batter rest for 10 minutes.

3. Preheat a non-stick pan on medium heat. Spray a small amount of fat-free non-stick spray.

4. Pour quarter cup portions of the batter in the pan. Cook for 1–2 minutes, or until the edges start to brown and bubble. Flip and cook for a further minute or two.

5. Serve the pancakes with fresh fruit.

Plant-Powered Lemon Oatmeal

LEVEL 1   **SERVINGS: 4**

Sweet oatmeal with apple pie flavors is common, but this savory and lemony oatmeal with nutritious greens and nuts is addictive, and gives a template for other types of savory oatmeal preparations. The possibilities are numerous.

 HEART HEALTH NOTE: Flavonoids in citrus affect NO by improving basal endothelial function. They enhance vascular function and decrease dysfunction by reducing oxidative stress. Naringin, a grapefruit flavonoid, provides an additional increase in endothelium flow.

2 cups whole oats (steel cut)

1 whole lemon, cut in half, juiced, and deseeded

1 teaspoon ground turmeric

1 teaspoon sumac powder (if available)

2 tomatillos, quartered

2 cups beet greens, washed and chopped

2 cups turnip greens, washed and chopped

¼ cup walnuts, chopped coarsely

6–8 cups water, more or less

1. Add all the ingredients except the oats and greens to the water and bring to a low simmer.

2. Stir in the oats and cover.

3. Stirring periodically, cook covered for as long the directions on the oats package says. This can be between 30 and 45 minutes.

4. Remove the lemon, chop it up finely and add it back to the pot. Add the greens, mix well, and cook for an additional 5 minutes.

5. Sprinkle chopped walnuts, before serving.

Silken Tofu & Tomato Scramble

LEVEL 1   SERVINGS: 4

The silken tofu definitely provides the texture of scrambled eggs. This recipe is inspired by a staple in India called "ande ka bhurji," which translates to "scrambled eggs." The remaining ingredients make this a very savory interpretation of scrambled eggs. The curry leaves are available in most South Asian grocery stores and are optional.

 HEART HEALTH NOTE: Soy proteins reduce oxidative stress and improve endothelial function along with reducing LDL levels. Isoflavones have demonstrated antioxidant properties which protect blood vessels from oxidative damage. Yet soy intake and CVD risk in pre- and post-menopausal women have opposing findings in major research studies. Only time will tell if soy can reduce the risk of CVD on adults.

½ teaspoon cumin seeds

2 medium tomatoes

1 teaspoon fresh ginger, minced

1 medium onion, chopped

1 teaspoon ground turmeric

½ teaspoon cayenne pepper (optional)

6–8 curry leaves (if available)

1 box (approximately 12 ounces) silken tofu

2 cups fresh leaf spinach

¼ cup fresh cilantro, chopped

Juice and zest of 1 lemon

Whole grain pita

1. On medium heat, roast the cumin seeds in a pan for 30 seconds.

2. Add the ginger and cook for 2 minutes to extract the flavor and aroma.

3. Next, add the ground turmeric, cayenne, onion, tomatoes, and curry leaves (if available) and cook for 5 minutes.

4. Now add the silken tofu and whisk into the mixture in the pan. Cook for 5 minutes.

5. Add the leaf spinach and mix well. As soon as it wilts, add the lemon zest and juice and finish with cilantro.

6. Serve with warm whole wheat pita.

Whole Grain Porridge

LEVEL 1   **SERVINGS: 4 / SERVING SIZE: 1 CUP**

Porridge can be sweet or savory. In this recipe, the assortment of whole grains, fruit, and nuts makes for a comforting and highly nutritious breakfast, year-round.

 HEART HEALTH NOTE: Whole grains contain the endosperm, germ, and bran, and have higher amounts of dietary fiber, magnesium and phytochemicals. High fiber helps to reduce total serum and low-density lipoprotein cholesterol concentrations. High fiber grains include rye, whole barley, hulled barley and bulgar.

1 sprig fresh thyme, leaves picked and chopped

1 bay leaf

½ cup dried or fresh cranberries

1 cinnamon stick or ½ teaspoon ground cinnamon

1 cup fat-free soymilk

2 tablespoons light date powder

3–4 cups water

½ cup pearl barley

½ cup whole oats (steel cut)

½ cup wild rice

1 cup whole corn

¼ cup chopped walnuts

Juice and zest of 1 orange

1. Add the thyme, bay leaf, cranberries, cinnamon, soymilk, and orange to the water and bring to a simmer in a heavy bottomed pot or pan.

2. Stir in the oats, barley, rice, and corn. Mix well.

3. Cover and cook on a low simmer, stirring periodically.

4. After about 40 minutes, add the walnuts and serve.

Breakfast Burrito

LEVEL 1   **SERVINGS: 4**

Who doesn't like a good breakfast burrito? As an addition to the filling described in the method below, you may also include a breakfast scramble with silken tofu (see page 65) inside the burrito for a familiar egg-like texture, without the saturated fats.

 HEART HEALTH NOTE: Onion flavonoids, called quercetin, increase NO production, improve endothelial function and help with diabetic vascular complications.

1 15-ounce can black beans, drained, rinsed

2 medium red onions, chopped

¼ cup red wine vinegar

2 cloves garlic, minced

2 tablespoons Adobo Seasoning (see page 245)

2 medium-sized ripe tomatoes, chopped

1 green pepper, cored and chopped

2 cups fresh spinach

1 cup shredded cabbage

1 lime

4 whole wheat tortilla

1 cup seedless cucumber, chopped

1 jalapeno, chopped (optional)

½ cup chopped fresh cilantro

1 avocado, chopped

1. In a bowl, mix the beans, half the onions, red wine vinegar, garlic, and adobo spice blend. Allow the mixture to sit for a total of 20 minutes, stirring periodically.

2. In a separate bowl, mix the tomatoes, other half of onions, zest and juice of the lime, cucumbers, cilantro, and jalapeno. Allow it to sit for 10 minutes.

3. Wrap the tortillas in foil and heat in a 350°F oven for 10 minutes to soften the tortillas.

4. Assemble the burritos with the black bean mixture, salsa fresca, and a fourth of the chopped avocado.

Pinto Beans Chilaquiles

LEVEL 2   SERVINGS: 4

Chilaquiles is a popular breakfast in Mexico. The word chilaquiles refers to an ancient Aztec word meaning "chilis and greens." Here, we use pinto beans to fortify the dish.

 HEART HEALTH NOTE: Soluble and insoluble fibers improve cardiovascular risk factors, such as blood pressure control and healthy gut biome. Most American adults only consume 16 grams per day of fiber, resulting in more than 90 percent of people falling short of adequate fiber intake. Because pinto beans have elevated fiber concentrations, even small increases in bean consumption allow for notable improvement to fiber and profound CVD resilience.

6 yellow corn tortillas

1 15-ounce can pinto beans (no-sodium), drained and rinsed

1 15-ounce can of crushed tomatoes, no-sodium

1 medium onion

½ teaspoon cumin powder

1 teaspoon dried Mexican oregano

1-inch piece, unsweetened dark chocolate, chopped up

1 teaspoon paprika

¼ cup red wine vinegar

1 lime

1 ripe avocado

1 cup fresh cilantro

½ cup water

1. Stack the tortillas and cut into 8 wedges each for a total of 48 triangles.

2. Bake the tortillas on a baking sheet in a 350°F oven until they get crisp. This will take 10–15 minutes. Set aside.

3. In a saucepan, roast the onion for 1 minute before adding the half the cumin, oregano, and paprika.

4. Roast for another 2 minutes before adding the tomatoes, zest and juice of the lime, and water.

5. Cook on medium for 5 minutes.

6. Blend the sauce with half of the fresh cilantro to a relatively smooth sauce.

7. In a sauté pan, heat the beans and chocolate. Add the remaining cumin, oregano, paprika, and red wine vinegar and cook for 5 minutes.

8. Add the tortilla crisps and pour in the tomato sauce. Stir quickly to coat all the ingredients.

9. Garnish with fresh avocado and cilantro.

Buckwheat Banana Pancakes

LEVEL 2   SERVINGS: 4

Buckwheat is a nutty and flavorful whole grain with many heart-health and anti-inflammatory benefits. By roasting the bananas, one intensifies its natural sugars making them even more delicious.

 HEART HEALTH NOTE: Buckwheat intake provides protective effects against hypertension, total cholesterol and LDL-cholesterol and cardiovascular diseases. It is a good source of gluten-free protein and fiber and has a low glycemic index, along with having 60% less fat than quinoa. The amino-acid profile, nutritional quality, and antioxidant capacity are all significantly improved in comparison with the wheat.

1 cup buckwheat flour

¼ cup all-purpose flour

1 egg equivalent of flaxseed gel (see page 23)

½ cup oat milk or soymilk

1 tablespoon apple cider vinegar

1 teaspoon vanilla extract

2 ripe bananas, thick slices

1 lemon, juice and zest

¼ cup walnuts, chopped coarsely

Non-stick, fat-free cooking spray

1. In a bowl, mix the flours, flaxseed gel, vanilla extract, lemon zest, and oat milk or soymilk. Allow the batter to rest for 15 minutes.

2. Mix the sliced bananas, vanilla extract, vinegar and spread on a non-stick baking sheet. Roast in a 350°F oven for 30 minutes or until the bananas are lightly golden brown.

3. Heat a non-stick pan on medium heat before spraying a small amount of non-stick, fat-free cooking spray on the heated pan. Ladle 2 ounces of batter in the center of the pan. Move the pan to form a circle of even thickness and cook for 2–3 minutes, before flipping. Cook for another couple of minutes. Continue until all the batter is used.

4. Serve the pancakes warm with a dollop of roasted banana and a sprinkle of walnuts.

Heart-Healthy Smoothie

LEVEL 1   **SERVINGS: 4**

Theoretically, one could blend any collection of heart-healthy fruits and vegetables. This version achieves a flavorful balance while providing an exciting start to one's morning.

 HEART HEALTH NOTE: Spinach contains high concentrations of nitrates, ultimately increasing NO and cardiac perfusion.

1 cup blueberries

1 tablespoon honey

Juice and zest of 1 lemon

1 cup kale with some stems, washed

2 cups spinach, washed

¼ cup mint leaves, washed

¼ cup walnuts

1. Blend the lemon juice, honey, and blueberries.

2. Add the remaining ingredients, push down, and add a touch of water (if needed) to achieve a smooth texture.

Whole Wheat Crepes with Strawberries

LEVEL 2   **SERVINGS: 4**

Traditionally, crêpes are made with melted butter and eggs. This recipe avoids both.

 HEART HEALTH NOTE: Kamut is a variety of ancient wheat grain that has been shown to significantly reduce the inflammatory cell signalers IL-6 and Tumor Necrosis Factor-α. TNF-α has also been known to increase reactive oxygen species levels and decrease nitric oxide production in blood vessels, which can lead to endothelial dysfunction.

- 1½ cups whole wheat flour
- 1 tablespoon cornstarch
- ½ teaspoon granulated sugar
- 1 teaspoon date powder
- ½ teaspoon baking powder
- 1 cup almond milk
- 1 cup soda water
- 1 teaspoon vanilla extract
- 2 cups fresh or frozen strawberries
- 1 star anise
- Juice and zest of 1 lemon

1. Mix the berries with the granulated sugar, lemon juice and zest, and star anise. Hold until crepes are ready.

2. In a bowl, whisk the flour, cornstarch, and sugar.

3. Slowly whisk in the soda water and almond milk. Allow the batter to rest for 15 minutes.

4. Heat a non-stick pan to medium heat.

5. Spray a small amount of fat-free, non-stick cooking spray.

6. Add ⅓ cup of batter to the pan. Pick up the pan and rotate it to nudge the batter into a thin circle.

7. Cook until the top looks dry. Using a spatula, turn over the crepe and cook on the other side for about 45 seconds.

8. Store without stacking.

9. Serve two small crepes with a serving of macerated strawberries.

Southwest-Style Oatmeal

LEVEL 1   SERVINGS: 4

This recipe deviates from the conventional sweet version of breakfast oatmeal, showing the versatility of grains and vegetables.

 HEART HEALTH NOTE: The quercetin found in onions increases NO, increases endothelial function, and helps with diabetic vascular complications.

1 small onion

1 jalapeño, chopped

½ cup carrots, small diced

½ cup black beans

Juice and zest of 1 lemon

1 tablespoon Creole Seasoning (see page 247)

1 teaspoon cumin powder

4 cups unsalted vegetable stock

1 cup coarse oatmeal

2 cups assorted chopped greens like kale, spinach, mustard greens, Swiss chard

¼ cup chopped walnuts

1. In a shallow pot, add the onion, jalapeño, carrot, black beans, lemon juice and zest, and spices to the vegetable stock. Bring to a low simmer.

2. Add the oatmeal, stirring to incorporate.

3. Cover and reduce the heat to low. Cook for about 20 minutes.

4. Add the greens and cook for another 10 minutes. Mix well.

5. Garnish with chopped walnuts.

Lentil & Pepper Pancake

LEVEL 1   **SERVINGS: 4**

Pesarattu is a green mung bean savory crêpe, a favorite of my mother's. This recipe is inspired by that memory and provides a canvas for a wide variety of variations and toppings.

HEART HEALTH NOTE: Lentils are plant-based protein-rich foods with vitamins and minerals such as potassium, phosphorus, thiamin, folate, magnesium, and calcium.

½ cup red lentils, washed and soaked in water for 10 minutes

½ cup white rice, washed and soaked in water for 10 minutes

Juice and zest of 1 lemon

½ teaspoon turmeric powder

½ teaspoon baking powder

1 small onion, diced

1 small jalapeño, de-seeded and chopped

Non-fat, non-stick cooking spray, as needed

1. Drain the lentils and rice, reserving 2 cups of the soaking liquid.

2. Using a powerful blender, blend the lentils, rice, lemon juice and zest, turmeric powder, and baking powder using a small amount of the soaking liquid. Add enough liquid during the blending to achieve a thick and smooth texture for the batter.

3. Leave the batter at room temperature for an hour.

4. Heat a non-stick pan to medium heat, spray a thin film of non-stick spray, and ladle about 3 ounces of batter in the center of the pan. Move the pan in a circular motion to spread the batter to a larger circle. Sprinkle some onion and jalapeño on the pancake.

5. Once the edges start to brown and the top bubbles and becomes opaque, flip the pancake. Cook for another 2–3 minutes.

6. Serve the pancakes with your favorite salsa or sauce.

Breakfast Sausage with Heart-Healthy Gravy

LEVEL 3   **SERVINGS: 4**

Biscuits and gravy is a widely popular breakfast in the United States, especially in the southern states. Of course, traditional versions are very high in animal fats and sodium. Here, I have provided a recipe for a homemade breakfast sausage and a light, comforting gravy.

 HEART HEALTH NOTE: Lentils are polyphenol-rich and reduce blood pressure by angiotensin I-converting enzyme (ACE) inhibitor activity. Lentils actively reduce the total cholesterol, triglycerides, and low-density lipoprotein (LDL).

1 cup dried brown lentils

1 cup rolled oats

2 teaspoons paprika

1 tablespoon onion powder

1 teaspoon garlic powder

1 teaspoon fennel seeds

1 cup ground flaxseed

1 small onion, chopped

1 stick celery, chopped

4 cups water

3 cups vegetable broth, no-sodium

1 teaspoon ground sage

1 teaspoon Dijon mustard

½ cup nutritional yeast

¼ cup oat milk

1 bay leaf

2 tablespoons tapioca starch

1 tablespoon chopped parsley

1 lemon

SAUSAGE

1. Cook the lentils on medium heat in a saucepan with 3 cups of water for 15–20 minutes until most of the water is absorbed.

2. Drain the lentils of excess water and in a bowl, mix the cooked lentils, oats, paprika, ¼ cup nutritional yeast, garlic powder, fennel seeds, chopped onion, and chopped celery.

3. Mix the flaxseed meal and remaining water to make a gel. Allow the gel to rest for about 10 minutes before adding it to the lentil mixture.

4. Preheat the oven to 400°F. With your hands, make 12 equal-sized balls and then shape into patties. Place them on a baking sheet and bake for about 15 minutes until lightly browned.

GRAVY

1. Mix one cup of broth and the tapioca starch to make a slurry.

2. Mix the remaining two cups of broth with sage, mustard, remaining nutritional yeast, bay leaf, and oat milk in a saucepan and bring to a simmer.

3. Slowly pour on the slurry, whisking continuously until the gravy thickens.

4. Finish with the chopped parsley and squeeze the juice of 1 lemon and stir in the zest of the lemon.

ASSEMBLY

Serve three patties with about ¾ cup of gravy.

Breakfast Sandwich

LEVEL 2   **SERVINGS: 4**

A classic breakfast sandwich might include eggs, cheese, and perhaps, a sage-scented sausage. While store bought plant-based sausages are plentiful, they are highly processed and high in saturated fats. This recipe gives a clean and bright alternative to a classic breakfast sandwich.

 HEART HEALTH NOTE: Nutritional yeast is an inactive form of the yeast strain *Saccharomyces cerevisiae*. The yeast cells are killed during processing but contain 0g fat and 60g protein per 100g. A great source of vitamin B3, B6, B1, B2, folate, as well as cobalamin, deficiency of which leads to endothelial dysfunction.

1 block extra-firm tofu, pressed for 30 minutes, then cut into 4 slices

1 tablespoon Creole Seasoning (see page 247)

¼ cup nutritional yeast

¼ cup oat milk

1 teaspoon sodium free liquid smoke (optional)

1 large fresh tomato, sliced into 4 slices

1 cup watercress

1 tablespoon white balsamic vinegar

1 ripe avocado, smashed

4 whole wheat, low/no-sodium English muffins

1. In a bowl, marinate the pressed tofu slices in a mixture of the oat milk, nutritional yeast, creole spice blend, and liquid smoke for 30 minutes.

2. In a non-stick or cast-iron skillet, on medium heat, brown the tofu on both sides. This should take about 5 minutes on each side.

3. Toast the English muffins.

4. In a bowl, dress the watercress with the white balsamic vinegar.

5. Assemble the sandwiches by spreading avocado on both sides of each sandwich, followed by a slice of cooked tofu, tomato, and dressed watercress.

Breakfast Scramble

LEVEL 1   SERVINGS: 4

This recipe provides a familiar breakfast texture and format with the added benefit of heart health and versatility. It may be served with roasted potatoes or fat-free toast.

 HEART HEALTH NOTE: Ginger can significantly reduce atherosclerotic lesion areas, LDL cholesterol levels, and elevated activity in platelet aggregation. It can also reduce advanced glycation end-products (AGEs) associated with cooking techniques. AGEs can induce the crosslinking of collagen and cause vascular stiffening and the sticking of LDL particles to the artery walls.

1 package of silken tofu, drained

1 cup chopped spinach

1 cup chopped kale

1 teaspoon turmeric powder

1 teaspoon fresh ginger, minced

1 clove garlic, minced

1 jalapeño, de-seeded and chopped

Juice and zest of 1 lemon

1. Combine all the ingredients except the lemon juice and zest in a pan.

2. Cook covered on medium until the greens are wilted. This will take about 15 minutes. Uncover and continue cooking until most of the liquid has evaporated.

3. Add the lemon juice and zest.

4. Taste and adjust the acidity. Add a dash of more lemon juice, if preferred.

Kale Caprese Toast

LEVEL 1   SERVINGS: 4

Avocado toast has found its way into homes and restaurants as a decadently satis-fying breakfast and brunch option. This version builds on a standard version with the addition of Italian flavors and heart-healthy greens.

 HEART HEALTH NOTE: Avocado consumption leads to a significantly higher intake of fiber, MUFA, vitamins E and C, folate, magnesium, and potassium. It also significantly reduces the LDL:HDL ratio and lowers LDL. Compared to animal fats, avocados improve vasodilation and reduce inflammation.

4 cups chopped kale

4 large basil leaves, torn

1 jalapeño, de-seeded, chopped

2 medium ripe tomatoes, diced

2 tablespoons, aged balsamic vinegar

1 ripe avocado, de-seeded

2 cloves garlic, minced

4 slices sourdough or multigrain bread

1. In a bowl, soak the garlic in 1 tablespoon of balsamic vinegar for 10 minutes.

2. Add the avocado, basil, and jalapeño and smash to a spread with a fork.

3. Massage the kale with the remaining balsamic vinegar for a minute and add the tomatoes.

4. Toast the bread, spread the avocado mixture, and top with the kale-tomato salad.

Lunch

A CLEAN AND NUTRITIOUS LUNCH is an essential bridge between breakfast and dinner, making straightforward preparation key for effective meal planning. This section offers recipes for dishes that can be made quickly or prepared ahead of time, all while emphasizing fantastic flavor and heart-healthy ingredients.

Green-Powered Berry Salad

LEVEL 1   SERVINGS: 4

The grapefruit and basil in the dressing counter the richness of the avocado while complementing the brightness of the berries.

 HEART HEALTH NOTE: Arugula contains the highest amounts of nitrate and consequently influences nitrate intake significantly. Our salivary glands and oral bacteria play an essential role in converting nitrate ($NO3-$) to nitrite ($NO2-$) and finally to nitric oxide (NO). Nitric oxide aids in endothelial function to increase perfusion.

2 cups fresh spinach

2 cups watercress

2 cups arugula

1 cup kale, chopped

2 cups assorted berries

1 cup fresh basil

2 grapefruits (slices and juice separated)

1 teaspoon Dijon mustard

1 ripe avocado, cored and chopped

¼ cup date syrup

2 tablespoons walnuts, chopped

1. Wash and dry all greens.

2. In a food processor, make the dressing by blending the grapefruit juice, Dijon mustard, date syrup, and basil. Adjust the sweetness and acidity as you desire.

3. Toss the greens and berries gently with enough dressing, leaving some on the side.

4. Sprinkle the grapefruit slices and walnuts on each salad.

Garbanzo Salad
with Lemon Thyme Dressing

LEVEL 1   **SERVINGS: 4**

This recipe is one of my personal favorites for two reasons. One, because I love garbanzo beans and two, because I love the combination of lemon and thyme.

 HEART HEALTH NOTE: Chickpeas are rich sources of protein, fiber, and minerals. In addition, their compounds decrease the level of LDL cholesterol and triacylglycerols. They improve DNA-damage signaling and levels of TNF-α, which mediates cardiac injury.

2 small yellow squash, halved lengthwise

2 small zucchini, halved

1 large red onion, peeled and sliced into thick slices

1 bunch asparagus, bases trimmed

1 can garbanzo beans, no-sodium, drained and rinsed

½ cup apple cider vinegar

1 teaspoon date syrup (optional)

2 cups kale or spinach (optional)

2 tablespoons Dijon mustard

3 lemons, zest and juice

2 tablespoons fresh thyme (substitute dried if necessary)

¼ cup Italian parsley, chopped

Black pepper, as desired

1. In a bowl, mix the vinegar, mustard, lemon juice and zest, parsley, and black pepper. Adjust the flavor by adding some date syrup if desired.

2. Coat the vegetables with half the dressing and let them marinate for 30 minutes.

3. Grill the marinated vegetables until just tender, moving them around so they don't burn. Alternatively, they can also be roasted on a baking sheet in the oven at 350°F for 30 minutes.

4. Chop the cooked vegetables into large pieces, then mix them with the garbanzo and more dressing.

5. Serve each portion as is, or on some kale or spinach dressed lightly with the same dressing.

Apple, Kale, Arugula, Spinach & Grapes Salad with Lime & Ginger Dressing

LEVEL 1   **SERVINGS: 4**

This salad is a powerhouse of flavor and nutrition, the best of both worlds. It is important to either choose young and tender kale leaves and stems or to massage more mature kale with the dressing to tenderize the fibers. This salad keeps well in the fridge because kale is hearty.

 HEART HEALTH NOTE: Combining foods that work in different pathways can help to maximize the cardiac benefits of those foods. For example: in this recipe, kale, arugula, and spinach make use of the Nitrate-Nitrite-NO pathways, while epicatechins, a compound in apples and black grapes, stimulate NO and activate eNOS, therefore increasing vasodilation.

4 cups fresh kale, washed, dried, and chopped

2 cups arugula

2 cups fresh spinach

2 cups seedless red grapes

2 Granny Smith apples, cored and chopped

1 small red onion, sliced thinly

2 limes, juice and zest

1 tablespoon fresh ginger, chopped

¼ cup apple cider vinegar

1 tablespoon date syrup

1 tablespoon Dijon mustard

¼ cup walnuts

Black pepper, as desired

1. In a blender or food processor, combine the lime juice and zest, mustard, vinegar, date syrup, and some black pepper. Blend until smooth. This is the lime and ginger dressing.

2. In a bowl, pour half of the lime and ginger dressing over the kale and massage well with your hands. Allow this to sit for 5 minutes.

3. Assemble each serving of salad with apple, walnuts, onion, arugula, and spinach over the dressed kale. Pour a bit more dressing on top.

Seasonal Bruschetta

LEVEL 1   SERVINGS: 4

Many Italian restaurants serve bruschetta as an appetizer because it is a versatile and shareable option. The term 'seasonal' in this recipe refers to the notion that, by following a few basic principles, it is possible to create versions that celebrate the bounty of the seasons year-round, thus ensuring maximum flavor, nutrition, and enjoyment.

 HEART HEALTH NOTE: White beans, white kidney beans, and Cannellini beans are similar. They are a nearly-perfect food due to their high content of fiber, protein, vitamins, and prebiotics. They have been shown to protect against oxidative stress, reduce serum cholesterol and LDL, and prevent atherosclerotic lesions.

1 large ripe tomato, chopped

2 cans white beans, no-sodium, drained and rinsed

2 cups spinach, chopped

1 cup fresh arugula, chopped

¼ cup white balsamic vinegar

1 teaspoon fresh oregano leaves, chopped

¼ cup Pepperonata sauce (see page 227)

1 clove fresh garlic

¼ cup fresh basil, chopped

12 slices whole wheat or multi-grain sliced bread

Red chili flakes, as desired

1. In a bowl, smash the beans, spinach, arugula, vinegar, red chili flakes, and oregano.

2. Toast the bread halfway and rub the garlic clove on one side of each half-toasted bread. Continue toasting until golden brown.

3. To assemble each bruschetta, spread an even layer of the bean spread, followed by fresh tomato, and dollops of Pepperonata, chopped tomato, red chili flakes if desired, and fresh basil.

Cucumber, Tomato & Watermelon Salad

LEVEL 1

Traditional green goddess dressing, while delicious, is high in saturated fats because of the use of mayonnaise or sour cream. The nuts provide a richness to the dressing avoiding the need to include mayonnaise or sour cream. If you like a particular herb, feel free to double up on its amount.

HEART HEALTH NOTE: Watermelon contains L-arginine, a nitric oxide (NO) precursor, along with polyphenols and carotenoids. Seedless mini watermelons have higher amounts of lycopene.

- **2 medium ripe tomatoes, sliced into wedges**
- **2 cups ripe watermelon chunks**
- **2 cups English (or other seedless) cucumber, sliced**
- **1 15-ounce can garbanzo beans (no-sodium), drained and rinsed**
- **¼ cup fat-free, dairy free yogurt**
- **1 cup fresh basil**
- **1 cup fresh Italian parsley**
- **½ cup fresh chives**
- **½ cup green onion**
- **1 tablespoon Dijon mustard**
- **¼ cup cashew nuts**
- **2 tablespoons white balsamic vinegar**
- **Baby lettuce (like bibb and butter)**
- **Black pepper, as desired**

1. Blend the yogurt, basil, parsley, chives, green onion, mustard, cashew nuts, vinegar, and some black pepper in a blender or food processor. This is the green goddess dressing.

2. In a bowl, dress the tomato, cucumber, and garbanzo with half the dressing. Let the mixture sit for 10 minutes.

3. Meanwhile, assemble each serving of salad by lightly dressing the lettuces and watermelon with some dressing and spread a serving of the garbanzo, tomato, cucumber mixture on top.

Ancient Grains Salad with Sherry Vinegar Dressing

LEVEL 2   SERVINGS: 4

Not long after I created this salad at the beginning of our restaurant, it quickly rose to becoming one of the most popular dishes on the menu, period. Even sworn non-vegetarians found great comfort and satisfaction with ordering just this salad as a main course.

 HEART HEALTH NOTE: Arugula assists in boosting heart health by positively influencing nitrate intake. Our salivary glands and oral bacteria play an essential role in converting nitrate (NO3-) to nitrite (NO2-) and finally to nitric oxide (NO), which aids in endothelial function to increase perfusion.

1 cup farro

½ cup red quinoa, washed well by rubbing between palms under water, rinsed

½ cup barley

4 cups arugula

¼ cup cranberries

¼ cup sherry vinegar

2 tablespoons light date powder

1 teaspoon Dijon mustard

¼ cup walnuts, chopped

2 quarts water (to cook the grains)

Black pepper, as needed

Herbs de Provence spice blend (see page 246)

1. In a pot, bring the water to a boil and add the farro and barley. Simmer uncovered for about 20 minutes.

2. Add the quinoa to the same pot, cover, and continue simmering for another 20 minutes. The quinoa should have specks of white indicating that they are cooked.

3. Drain the cooked grains.

4. In a glass or stainless bowl, mix the vinegar, mustard, and date powder. Taste and adjust the acidity and sweetness to your liking.

5. Mix half the dressing with the cooked grains and the dress the arugula with the remaining half.

6. To assemble a salad, sprinkle a serving of cooked grains on a serving of dressed arugula.

7. Sprinkle each salad with cranberries and walnuts.

Garlic & White Bean Stew

LEVEL 1   **SERVINGS: 4**

Cannellini beans are luxuriously creamy. This is a simple soup but a great example of flavor through simplicity and good cooking technique.

 HEART HEALTH NOTE: Dark green leafy vegetables, such as rapini, are associated with increased plasma β-carotene levels and decreased systemic CRP levels over time.

1 small onion, finely chopped

1 small carrot, diced

1 celery stalk, finely chopped

2 garlic cloves, minced

2 cups rapini (aka broccoli rabe), chopped

1 tablespoon Tuscan Spice Blend (see page 243)

1 lemon, zest and juice

1 small can cannellini beans (no-sodium), drained and rinsed

1 small tomato, diced

2 cups vegetable stock or water

1 cup dry white wine

Black pepper, as desired

1. Start by roasting the mirepoix (onions, carrots, and celery) in a saucepan for about 5 minutes over medium heat.

2. Next, add the garlic and Tuscan spice blend. After 2 minutes, add the rapini, tomatoes and beans, and stew for 5 minutes.

3. Now add the wine and stock and simmer for 30 minutes.

4. Transfer a cup of the beans and some broth to a blender and puree before adding back to the soup or use an immersion blender to break down some of the beans and vegetables a bit. This provides body and deeper flavor to the soup.

5. Serve each serving of soup with some lemon juice and zest to be mixed in for added brightness.

Southwestern Pinto Bean, Poblano & Corn Chowder

LEVEL 1   SERVINGS: 4

The American Southwest has cornered the flavor market when it involves creations involving corn, beans, and capsicum, thanks in large part to the influence of Mexican culinary traditions coupled with a rich history of indigenous foods.

 HEART HEALTH NOTE: High circulating blood sugars cause oxidative stress, damaging the endothelium and affecting blood flow. Low glycemic foods appear to stabilize or reduce that damage. Most beans (such as pinto, black, kidney, and navy) have a low glycemic index.

1 can pinto beans (no-sodium), drained and rinsed

3 ears of corn with husk, shave kernels off cob

2 poblano peppers, cored and chopped finely

2 medium skin on potatoes, washed and chopped into medium chunks

1 large onion, cut into large pieces

1 stalk celery, diced

¼ cup roasted, unsalted pumpkin seeds, chopped coarsely

½ bunch cilantro, chop stems and leaves separately

4 cloves garlic, minced

2 bay leaves

2 teaspoons cumin powder

½ teaspoon cayenne powder

1 cup apple cider vinegar

1 quart water

Juice and zest of 1 lime

1. Add all the ingredients except the cilantro leaves to a pot and bring to a simmer. Taste the liquid and adjust the acidity.

2. Cook for about 45 minutes on a steady simmer, stirring occasionally.

3. Discard the bay leaves.

4. Transfer a third of the soup to a blender and pulse a few times. Return the processed batch back to the pot.

5. Serve with crushed pumpkin seeds, fresh cilantro, and a wedge of lime.

Vegetable Platter with Peanut Hummus

LEVEL 1   **SERVINGS: 4**

This is the kind of dish that is ideal for picnics, gatherings, or when you don't want to be fussy about your meal. Because the choice of vegetables can be from a wide list, it isn't imperative that you have very specific ones.

 HEART HEALTH NOTE: Legumes include green peas and beans, chickpeas, peanuts, clover, soybeans, dry beans, broad beans, dry peas, alfalfa, and lentils. High consumption of legumes is associated with a 10 percent decreased risk of CVD.

2 cups assorted roasted vegetables like cauliflower florets, broccoli florets, and turnips

2 cups assorted raw vegetables (crudité) like peppers, celery, carrots, and cucumber

2 cups, just cooked green peas

½ cup cooked, unsalted green peanuts (substitute dry roasted if necessary)

1 teaspoon dry roasted cumin powder

1 teaspoon sumac (if available)

¼ cup chopped fresh parsley

1 teaspoon sesame seeds

1 clove garlic, minced and soaked in the lemon juice

Black pepper, as desired

Juice and zest of 1 lemon

1. Prepare the portions of raw and roasted (unsalted, no oil) vegetables.

2. In a food processor, blend the cooked peas, peanuts, garlic with lemon juice and zest, cumin powder, sumac, and parsley to the desired consistency of hummus. Sprinkle some sesame seeds on each serving of hummus.

3. Serve the pea and peanut hummus with the raw and roasted vegetables.

Root Vegetable, Spinach & Tarragon Soup

LEVEL 1   **SERVINGS: 4**

This is a comforting soup with a rich mouthfeel, but without the guilt. I would recommend garnishes that provide a bright and acidic texture with a crisp texture — say a pickled relish and herb whole wheat croutons.

 HEART HEALTH NOTE: Increasing the consumption of Yellow-Orange-Red vegetables has been shown to decrease the risks of heart disease (but not stroke). These results, found across numerous studies, can vary; but eating these vegetables has never been found to have a negative impact on one's health.

- 1 medium turnip, chopped into small chunks
- 1 cup cored and chopped Granny Smith apple
- 1 medium parsnip, peeled and chopped into small chunks
- 1 medium potato, peeled and chopped into small chunks
- 1 medium sweet potato, peeled and chopped into small chunks
- 1 medium carrot, chopped into small chunks
- 3 cups fresh spinach
- 1 tablespoon dried tarragon
- 3 garlic cloves, minced
- 2 cups oat milk
- 1 cup dry white wine
- 1 quart water
- Ground black pepper, as desired

1. Heat a pot on medium heat and add the garlic. Cook for about 30 seconds.

2. Add the white wine and cook for a minute.

3. Add the water, all vegetables, apple, and tarragon.

4. Season with some black pepper and bring to a simmer. Cook covered until all vegetables are tender. This should take about 30 minutes.

5. With a hand blender, pulse the soup a bit to break it down. This thickens it naturally. Alternatively, blending a third of the soup and adding it back to the pot has the same effect.

6. Adjust the acidity. Add a squeeze of lemon, if desired.

Green Gazpacho Soup

LEVEL 1   SERVINGS: **4**

Gazpacho is a good catch-all for herbs and greens that may be wilting in your refrigerator. This is a delicious and vibrant soup with so much flavor and nutrition. As if that's not enough, it's one of the easiest to make.

 HEART HEALTH NOTE: Tomatillo, also called husk tomatoes, are related to the Indian gooseberry. Both are known for their heart-healthy antioxidant properties, but the Indian gooseberry with an antioxidant score of 261.53 millimoles (mmol)/100g dominates as one of the highest natural sources of antioxidants. In comparison, the blueberry's score is 9.24 (mmol)/100g.

½ cup kale

1 cup spinach

½ cup watercress

1 cup arugula

1 seedless skin-on cucumber, chopped

1 stick celery, chopped

½ cup green grapes with skin and seeds

1 medium green bell pepper, cored and chopped

2 medium tomatillo, quartered

½ cup fresh basil

¼ cup fresh cilantro

½ cup fresh parsley

3 cloves garlic, minced

2 tablespoons Dijon mustard

¼ cup Sherry vinegar

½ cup almonds, chopped

½ jalapeno (optional)

1 tablespoon date syrup

Water, as needed to blend to a thick consistency.

1. Mix the vinegar and garlic in a bowl and allow the mixture to be for 2 minutes.

2. Add the remaining ingredients, including the vinegar and garlic mixture and half the almonds to the blender and blend to a smooth consistency. Adjust the acidity per preference.

3. Serve in a bowl topped with a few almonds and fresh herbs of your choice.

Tunisian Sweet Potato & Lentil Stew

LEVEL 1   SERVINGS: 4

The cuisine in the city of Marrakech in Morocco, offers up the vast repertoire of dishes featuring legumes. Crossing over local giant Algeria, one arrives in Tunisia and her spectacular port towns. This soup could be just as easily claimed by Morocco, based on flavor profile alone. The addition of sweet potato balances the flavors, offers texture, and a wealth of health benefits.

HEART HEALTH NOTE: Dietary pulses, like lentils, are recommended by health authorities across the world for their nutritional value and effectiveness in helping with feeding people. They are a powerful tool in the global food supply and have been associated with improved LDL concentrations and systolic blood pressure.

1½ cups green or brown lentils

3 medium carrots, chopped

2 celery sticks, chopped

1 red onion, finely chopped

3 garlic cloves, finely chopped

2 medium potatoes, peeled and cubed

2 sweet potatoes, peeled, cubed

½ teaspoon ground cumin

½ teaspoon ground cinnamon

½ teaspoon cayenne pepper

3 cups vegetable stock, no-sodium

1 cup red wine vinegar

Water, as needed

Half a bunch of coriander, chopped

Juice and zest of 1 lemon

Black pepper, as desired

1. Add the lentils to about twice as much water. Cook until they are half done and set aside.

2. In a pot over medium heat, cook the onions, carrots, and celery until slightly brown and somewhat translucent.

3. Add garlic, stirring for few seconds.

4. Add the spices and potatoes and continue roasting, stirring constantly, until they become fragrant (about 2 minutes); then add the lentils, vinegar, and stock. Bring to a boil and skim any fat from the surface.

5. Reduce to a simmer and partly cover the pot. Continue cooking for about 30 minutes.

6. Partially blend the soup, thickening it naturally.

7. Adjust the acidity, then stir in the coriander, lemon zest, and lemon juice.

Black Bean and Butternut Squash Soup

LEVEL 1   SERVINGS: 4

Even though black beans and a sweeter squash like butternut lend themselves well to Southwestern and Mexican flavors, here, I give you a version that, if it wasn't for the notable addition of fresh ginger, is almost French.

 HEART HEALTH NOTE: Classic Native Americans foods, bean and butternut squash are a rich source of phenolic antioxidants which work to counter chronic oxidative stress of CVD. Frequently, they were combined with colored corn, and were widely known as the "three sisters crops."

2 cups black beans, canned, no-sodium, drained and rinsed

2 ripe medium (or 1 large) butternut squash

2 tablespoons minced fresh ginger

1 teaspoon fresh garlic, minced

1 medium red onion, small dice

½ teaspoon freshly grated nutmeg

1 tablespoon fresh tarragon, chopped

2 cups dry white wine

½ cup oat milk (optional)

Classic Bouquet Garni (see page 196)

Vegetable stock (no-sodium, preferably homemade), as needed

Water, as needed

1. Peel the butternut squash, scoop out the core, and cut into medium-sized pieces.

2. In a heavy-bottomed pot, cook the onion and fresh ginger for a couple of minutes.

3. Add the garlic and cook while stirring for about 1 minute.

4. Next, add the remaining ingredients except for the oat milk. Stir and check to make sure it's well-seasoned. Simmer on low-medium heat for 20 minutes. Blend to a smooth puree.

5. Finish with the oat milk (optional) and tarragon.

Grilled Peaches, Brown Rice & Arugula

LEVEL 1   SERVINGS: **8**

Not all fruit grills well, but peaches while still slightly firm take to grilling really well. This is a simple recipe with a complex flavor.

 HEART HEALTH NOTE: The health benefits of polyphenols have been attributed to their antioxidant capacity as free radical scavengers. Quercetin is a plant flavonoid found in peaches, buckwheat, grapes, onions and citrus. They have vasodilative effects and reduces adhesion molecules during a clot or heart attack.

2 cups cooked brown rice

4 semi-ripe peaches, de-seeded and halved

1 medium red onion, sliced thinly

4 cups arugula

¼ cups walnuts

¼ cup fresh basil

½ cup Lime & Ginger Dressing (see page 72)

Black pepper, as desired

1. In a bowl, dress the peaches using half of the dressing and allow them to marinate for 20 minutes.

2. While the peaches are marinating, mix the remaining dressing into the cooked brown rice, onion, walnuts, black pepper, and basil.

3. Grill the peaches until they soften a bit. Allow them to cool a bit and chop into desired sized pieces.

4. Serve the peaches on a bed of arugula and brown rice mixture.

Assorted Greens Stew

LEVEL 1   **SERVINGS: 4**

Greens are prolific in the fall where we live. Every community supported agriculture (CSA) ration is filled with a wide variety of them. Each green is unique. However, when combined in this simple way, the end result is a beautiful marriage of earth and chlorophyll. One may add cooked grains like farro or quinoa to really make this a meal in a bowl.

HEART HEALTH NOTE: Rapini, escarole, collard and mustard greens are best utilized on the Nitrate (NO_3^-) → Nitrite (NO_2^-) → Nitric oxide (NO) pathways, ultimately facilitating vasodilation.

3 cups kale, cleaned, chopped

2 cups broccoli rabe (rapini), cleaned, chopped

2 cups escarole, cleaned, chopped

1 cup collard greens, cleaned, chopped

1 cup mustard greens, cleaned, chopped

1 tablespoon fresh ginger root, minced

4 cloves fresh garlic, minced

1 large yellow onion, diced

1 teaspoon cumin powder

1 teaspoon coriander powder

2 quarts no-sodium vegetable stock

1 cup apple cider vinegar

2 cups oat milk (optional)

Black pepper, as desired

1. In a large, heavy-bottomed pot, roast the onions until golden brown and slightly translucent.

2. Add the fresh ginger and garlic and cook for 1 minute.

3. Add the cumin, coriander, and some pepper. Stir for a minute.

4. Add the greens. Toss in the pot until they start to wilt. This may take about 5 minutes. Cover the pot if necessary.

5. Add the stock and vinegar. Bring to a simmer and cook for about 45 minutes.

6. Finish with oat milk (optional). Blend partially.

7. Serve with cooked brown rice or multigrain bread.

Summer Rolls with Sweet & Sour Sauce

LEVEL 1   SERVINGS: 4

Many Thai and Vietnamese restaurants offer summer rolls as an appetizer. There is no denying how light and fresh these can be. Here, I include an additional textural component—asparagus. If you have never made summer rolls before, you will quickly find out how easy they are, once you find your rhythm for handling the rice paper. Note that the rice paper is already cooked. It only needs to be made pliable by dipping into warm water and spreading out, carefully. After that, the process is identical to making a burrito.

 HEART HEALTH NOTE: A bioactive natural compound present in asparagus may provide inhibitory activity against angiotensin-converting enzymes (ACEs) due to its sulfur content. ACE controls blood pressure by regulating the volume of fluids in the body.

12 asparagus spears, ends trimmed, each cut into thirds (36 pieces)

1 box semi-firm tofu, drained well and cut unto 12 strips

1 seedless cucumber, leave skin on, cut into thin strips

2 carrots, leave skin on, shred or cut into thick strips

4 leaves romaine lettuce, chopped

12 rice papers

¼ cup fresh mint leaves

¼ cup fresh basil leaves

½ cup fresh cilantro leaves

2 tablespoons date syrup

½ cup rice wine vinegar

¼ cup fresh orange juice

1 teaspoon fresh ginger, grated or minced

Any type of medium-hot green chili, chopped (optional)

Water for blanching asparagus

1. Cook the asparagus in boiling water for 30 seconds, before draining, and running cold water on them to cool them quickly.

2. Mix date syrup, vinegar, green chili, orange juice, and ginger in a bowl.

3. Read the directions on the rice paper package. Typically, soaking each wrapper in hot water briefly will rehydrate it quickly.

4. Carefully spread each softened wrapper on a flat surface.

5. Place a piece of tofu, 3 pieces of asparagus, lettuce, carrots, cucumber, mint, basil, and cilantro in the center-bottom of each wrapper. Fold the bottom over, pull in the sides, and continue rolling tightly by keeping the tension on the wrapper. Store the rolls with the seam down.

6. If you tear the wrapper or it's too loose, no worries. Eat it anyway and continue forward. Practice makes perfect.

7. After all rolls have been assembled, the sweet and sour dipping sauce should be ready.

Ultimate Plant-Based Chili

LEVEL 2   SERVINGS: 4

Every cuisine I know has a low and slow stew. Chili isn't exactly a stew, but one does stew it down. This version is packed with flavor, comfort, nutrition, and decadence.

 HEART HEALTH NOTE: Apple cider vinegar (ACV) contains a variety of flavonoids, such as gallic acid and catechin. ACV consumption significantly decreases serum TC concentrations. In addition, there is evidence to suggest a trend towards its significantly reducing serum TG levels.

1 cup firm tofu, crumbled

1 medium onion, chopped

1 stick celery, chopped

1 medium carrot, chopped

1 jalapeno, chopped

4 cloves garlic, minced

½ cup cremini mushrooms, chopped

2 cups dry red wine

1 small can red beans (no-sodium), drained and rinsed

1 small can white beans (no-sodium), drained and rinsed

1 small can crushed tomatoes (no-sodium)

1 tablespoon Adobo Seasoning (see page 245)

1 teaspoon garlic powder

1 tablespoon onion powder

1 teaspoon mustard powder

1 teaspoon cayenne pepper, more or less

2 cups apple cider vinegar

½ cup scallions, chopped

Water, as needed

1. In a heavy-bottomed pot, brown the tofu. Remove and set aside.

2. Add the onions, celery, carrots, jalapeno and sweat for about 10 minutes.

3. Add the minced garlic and cook for about a minute.

4. Add the beans, tomatoes, Adobo spice blend, garlic powder, onion powder, mustard powder, cayenne pepper and cook for about a minute.

5. Add the mushrooms and the browned tofu back in and stir well.

6. Add the wine and vinegar and cook for 5 minutes.

7. Next, add all the remaining ingredients except the scallions. Stir well.

8. Adjust the acidity as preferred. Bring to a simmer, cover, and cook on medium for 30 minutes.

9. For the last 10 minutes, remove the lid and simmer uncovered.

10. Blend a cup of the chili in a food processor and add it back to the pot. Mix well.

11. Finish by topping with chopped scallions.

Mushroom & Cabbage Slaw

LEVEL 1   SERVINGS: 4

This Thai-inspired slaw may be enjoyed on its own, as a side item, or as a vehicle to add tofu or cooked beans for a lunch or dinner option.

 HEART HEALTH NOTE: Sulforaphane (SFN) is a sulfur-rich compound found in cabbage and plays a cardioprotective role due to its antioxidant and anti-inflammatory properties. Reductions in chronic inflammation and oxidative stress improve coronary flow and decrease atherosclerosis and hypertension. When preparing cabbage, both raw and severely heat-treated cabbage display reduced potential health benefits, while mild cooking of cabbages, such as mild steaming and gentle roasting, maximizes SFN beneficial benefits.

2 cloves garlic, minced

1 teaspoon fresh ginger, minced

1 tablespoon raw honey

Juice and zest of 2 limes

Juice of 1 orange

1 tablespoon unsalted peanut butter

1 tablespoon rice wine vinegar

2 cups cremini mushrooms, cleaned and destemmed, sliced thickly

2 cups Napa cabbage, shredded or sliced thinly

1 cup red cabbage, sliced thinly

¼ cup unsalted peanuts

1 jalapeño, de-seeded and chopped

½ cup cilantro with stems, chopped

½ cup fresh basil leaves, chopped

1. To make the dressing, in a glass bowl mix the garlic, ginger, honey, juice plus zest of both citrus, peanut butter, and vinegar well.

2. Bake the mushrooms on a sheet tray for 15 minutes in a 350°F oven.

3. Toss the cabbage with the dressing, adding as much as desired. Set aside for 15 minutes as the mushrooms are roasting.

4. Finish by adding the herbs, mushrooms, and peanuts. Add more dressing as desired.

Curried Garbanzo & Roasted Sweet Potato Salad

LEVEL 1   SERVINGS: 4

To curry something typically involves more than just adding a spice blend. However, garbanzo beans have a propensity to take on the flavors of a spice blend deeply with only a bit of cooking.

 HEART HEALTH NOTE: High total protein decreases all-cause mortality, while high plant proteins significantly decrease both all-cause mortality and cardiovascular deaths. When it comes to amino acids, beans are rich in lysine and low in the sulfur-containing amino acid methionine. (Rice is methionine-rich, hence why you can add rice to the beans!)

2 medium sweet potatoes, washed and cut into medium-sized pieces

2 cans no-sodium garbanzo beans, drained and rinsed

2 cloves garlic, minced

1 tablespoon Garam Masala (see page 236)

¼ cup white balsamic vinegar, divided

4 cups chopped kale

1. Preheat the oven to 375°F.

2. Toss the sweet potatoes, garbanzo, garlic, spice blend, and half the vinegar in a bowl.

3. Spread the mixture in a uniform single layer on a baking sheet and bake for about 30-40 minutes or until the sweet potatoes are tender.

4. Massage the kale with the remaining vinegar and set aside.

5. After the roasted mixture cools down, mix in the kale and serve.

Quinoa & Black Bean Burger

LEVEL 1   **SERVINGS: 4**

There are a multitude of premade veggie burgers on the market, but this version will leave both vegetarians as well as non-vegetarians satisfied!

 HEART HEALTH NOTE: Quinoa packs a protein punch! Not only does it have a balanced mix of amino acids like milk protein, but its proteins are also readily digestible and usable by the body.

1 large red onion, chopped

1 medium carrot, peeled, grated

2 tablespoons fresh garlic, minced

1 (12-ounce) can black beans, rinsed and drained well

1 cup cooked quinoa

¼ cup unsalted cashew nuts

¼ cup flax seed soaked in warm water

1 poblano or jalapeño pepper, chopped

1 tablespoon Creole Seasoning (see page 247)

1 teaspoon cumin powder

Unseasoned panko breadcrumbs, as needed

1. In a food processor, coarsely blend all the ingredients except the breadcrumbs. Transfer to a bowl.

2. Add enough breadcrumbs so that the mixture is dry enough to make patties. Make four patties.

3. Bake the patties in a 350°F oven for 10–15 minutes, turning once.

4. Enjoy burgers on whole wheat or multigrain buns with your favorite unsalted and fat-free condiments.

Caprese Panini

This sandwich—accompanied by a warm bowl of soup—makes for a perfectly tasty, healthy, and filling meal.

 HEART HEALTH NOTE: Cashews are packed with magnesium, they fuel the body's antioxidant defenses, making them a delicious way to protect your heart. For a bonus, spinach, whole grains, and dried fruits join the magnesium squad.

1 cup no-sodium white beans, drained and rinsed

¼ cup unsalted cashews

1 tablespoon Tuscan Spice Blend (see page 243)

Juice and zest of 1 lemon

¼ cup basil leaves

1 clove garlic

8 slices of sourdough, multigrain, or whole wheat bread

2 ripe tomatoes, cored and sliced into ¼-inch slices

4 leaves of Romaine or red leaf lettuce

Freshly ground black pepper

1. Blend the beans, cashews, spice blend, lemon juice and zest, basil, garlic, and black pepper to form a coarse, but spreadable spread.

2. Toast two slices of bread, spread the bean spread, and assemble each sandwich with tomato and lettuce.

3. Weigh down with a heavy pan and toast both sides in a pan. Alternatively, use a panini press.

Green Tomato & Black Bean Torta Sandwich

LEVEL 2   SERVINGS: 4

One of the finest tortas I've had was at *Tortas Frontera* by Rick Bayless at Chicago's O'Hare International Airport. It made such an impression on me that as fast as I could scarf it down, the seed had already been planted to include my interpretation in a future book. That was a few years ago while I was returning from the annual James Beard Awards at Lyric Opera House. As an invited chef for the after-party, I created a Mumbai street-food dish accented with leche de tigre, date-tamarind chutney, and salsa verde.

 HEART HEALTH NOTE: Avocado consumption leads to a significantly higher intake of fiber, MUFA, vitamins E and C, folate, magnesium, and potassium. It also significantly reduces the LDL:HDL ratio and lowers LDL. Compared to animal fats, avocados improve vasodilation and reduce inflammation.

1 large can black beans, pre-cooked, drained, and rinsed

½ cup Sofrito (see page 224)

2 tablespoons Adobo Seasoning (see page 245)

3 tablespoons aquafaba

½ cup watercress greens

¼ cup picked fresh cilantro leaves and tender stems

2 ripe avocados, thinly sliced

4 torta (bolillo) rolls (available at any Mexican bakery) or a demi-baguette

2 large green tomatoes, sliced into 8 slices

Juice from 1 lime

Black pepper, as desired

1. In a bowl, combine the black beans and sofrito.

2. Make a compound spread by mixing half the adobo blend and the aquafaba.

3. Make a salad with the watercress, cilantro, some pepper, and juice of half a lime.

4. Season the green tomatoes with the other half of the adobo blend and either grill until just soft or place on a baking sheet and roast in the oven for 15 minutes.

5. Toast the bread and assemble each torta by spreading the adobo spread on both sides, adding a layer of sofrito-enhanced black beans, green tomato, avocado slices, and the watercress-cilantro salad.

6. Squeeze a bit more lime juice on top of the filling and serve immediately.

Mumbai Chutney Sandwich

LEVEL 2   SERVINGS: 4

This omnipresent sandwich is available all over Mumbai: at street carts, in sit-down cafes, and in many homes. My parents worked full-time and took turns cooking for the family. On the rare occasion when they just weren't up to it and felt uninspired, we were treated to a modest version of this sandwich, and it was "chutney sandwich night" at home. Hari loved chutney sandwich night. I would often be tasked with procuring the provisions for said sandwiches. The version below is more representative of ones found on the street.

HEART HEALTH NOTE: Beets, classified as one of the best sources of high levels of antioxidants (outside of the Indian gooseberry and tomatillo) contain phytochemicals, flavonoids, polyphenols, and inorganic nitrate (NO3-), to name just a few of their benefits. In the nitric oxide (NO) pathway, NO dilates all types of vascular vessels and protects platelet aggregation and leukocyte adhesion.

1 cup smashed cooked or canned garbanzo

2 tablespoons red wine vinegar

8 slices sturdy, whole wheat or whole grain bread, sliced

1 cup Salsa Verde (see page 218)

2 Yukon gold or white potatoes, boiled and sliced

1 red beet, cooked and sliced

1 large ripe tomato, sliced thinly

1 cucumber (seedless), sliced

1 medium red onion, sliced thinly

Black pepper, as desired

1. Mix the smashed garbanzo and red wine vinegar in a bowl for 10 minutes.

2. Meanwhile, toast the bread in a toaster or oven to a golden brown.

3. For each spread the smashed garbanzo on both sides.

4. Next, spread the salsa verde on both sides.

5. Assemble the sandwich with layers of potato, beet, tomato, cucumber, onion, and a uniform sprinkle of black pepper.

Stuffed Acorn Squash

LEVEL 1   **SERVINGS: 4**

In general, winter squashes offer a delicious and versatile vehicle for filling with decadent fillings. One may also use commonly available butternut squash. Delicata squash, if available is an excellent choice as well.

 HEART HEALTH NOTE: The humble acorn squash was a Mesoamerican power-house high in fiber, vitamin C, potassium, and magnesium, all of which contribute to heart health by supporting healthy blood pressure levels and reducing the risk of heart disease.

1 medium acorn squash

1 cup no-sodium garbanzo beans, drained and rinsed

1 tablespoon Adobo Seasoning (see page 245)

1 medium tomato, diced

1 medium onion, diced

2 sticks celery, diced

¼ cup white balsamic vinegar

½ cup chopped cilantro

1. Trim the ends of the squash and cut four uniform slices, leaving the skin on. With a spoon, scoop out the seeds and fibers.

2. Roast the squash slices in a 375°F oven for about 40 minutes or until browned and soft.

3. While the squash is roasting, in a bowl, combine the remaining ingredients and set aside.

4. Once the squash slices are out of the oven, turn them over and allow them to cool a bit.

5. Fill the hollowed-out squash slices with the garbanzo salad to enjoy a tasty and nutritious dish.

Sweet Potato, Farro, Grilled Onion & Watercress

LEVEL 1   **SERVINGS: 4**

The most time-consuming aspect of this recipe is the cooking of the farro. On your prep day, along with cooking some beans, consider cooking some grains as well. Enough for a few days so that you can incorporate them into your meals quickly and without much pre-planning.

 HEART HEALTH NOTE: The quercetin found in onions increases NO, increases endothelial function and helps with diabetic vascular complications.

1 cup cooked farro
   (2 parts water, 1-part
   farro, 1 cup dry
   white wine)

2 medium-sized skin-on
   sweet potatoes, sliced
   and oven roasted at
   350°F for 30 minutes

1 large, red or sweet
   white onion, large
   slices

1 cup celery, thin slices

¼ cup Lemon Thyme
   Dressing (see page 71)

4 cups, watercress,
   washed and dried

Black pepper, as desired

1. Marinate the onion in a tablespoon of dressing for 15 minutes and grill or roast with the sweet potatoes.

2. In a bowl, toss the cooked sweet potato, celery slices, onion, and cooked farro with a tablespoon of dressing. Allow the mixture to sit for 10 minutes.

3. Dress the watercress with the remaining dressing, black pepper, and one serving of the sweet potato mixture.

Ultimate Burger

There are a multitude of premade veggie burgers on the market, but this version can be customized for all the benefits of a whole food, plant-based diet coupled with a satisfying experience.

 HEART HEALTH NOTE: The U.S. Dietary Guidelines recommend eating about 3 cups of legumes per week. So, if you eat about ½ cup of beans daily, you'll meet the weekly goal. They are a good protein source, low in saturated fat and contribute to viscous (soluble) fiber intake as part of the Portfolio Diet.

12 ounce can black beans, drained and rinsed well

12 ounce can red beans, drained and rinsed well

1 cup grated red beet

2 poblano peppers, chopped

6-ounce firm tofu, cubed

2 tablespoons Creole Seasoning (see page 247)

1 large red onion, chopped

2 tablespoons fresh garlic, minced

2 tablespoons fresh flat-leaf parsley, chopped

1 tablespoon fresh garlic, minced

1 teaspoon smoked paprika

¼ cup flax seed soaked in warm water

Panko breadcrumbs, no-sodium, as needed

Black pepper, as needed

Whole wheat or whole grain hamburger buns

Preferred burger toppings (low-sodium and fat free)

1. Preheat oven to 350°F and, on a baking sheet, roast the beans, beet, peppers, and tofu, seasoned a bit with creole spice blend for 45 minutes.

2. After all ingredients have cooled, mix all the ingredients except the breadcrumbs, in a large bowl. Add enough breadcrumbs to be able to form about four ½-inch-thick patties. If you are able to make more, store in the fridge for another day or freeze.

3. To finish, toast the patties on a baking sheet in the oven, or in a pan, until golden brown on both sides.

4. Top with your cheese alternative (see pages 199–201), if preferred, and assemble your burgers with the low-sodium, fat-free, plant-based accompaniments that you prefer. It will be enjoyable to dress the lettuce or greens with red wine vinegar.

Cauliflower Tacos

LEVEL 2   **SERVINGS: 4**

Roasted cauliflower and white beans kissed with bright and herbaceous flavors makes for a fantastic taco, enchilada, and burrito filling.

 HEART HEALTH NOTE: Quercetin is the major flavonoid found in cauliflower and is used to treat inflammatory disorders and cardiovascular diseases. Quercetin also reduces the overproduction of ROS and prevents myocardial cell injury. It may also inhibit the release of pro-inflammatory cytokines.

4 cups cauliflower florets

2 tablespoons Adobo Seasoning (see page 245)

1 large can of any type of white beans, drained and rinsed well

¼ cup Salsa Verde (see page 218)

1 medium onion, minced

1 jalapeno, minced (more, if preferred)

2 cups chopped spinach or kale

2 Granny Smith apples, shaved or grated

1 cup shredded or sliced red radish

1 tablespoon red wine vinegar

¼ cup fresh cilantro

1 lime

8 medium whole wheat tortillas

1. On a baking sheet, season the cauliflower with 1 tablespoon of adobo spice blend and roast the cauliflower in a 350°F oven for 30 minutes.

2. While the cauliflower is roasting, in a bowl, mix the beans, onion, salsa verde, jalapeno, and the remaining adobo.

3. After the cauliflower has roasted and softened, the tacos are ready to be assembled.

4. If using kale, massage it with the red wine vinegar. If using spinach, dress it with the red wine vinegar.

5. Warm the tortillas until they are soft and pliable.

6. Assemble each taco with the bean mixture, roasted cauliflower, dressed greens, apple, and radish.

7. If desired, squeeze some lime juice on each taco before enjoying.

Lentil Sloppy Joe

Admittedly, Indians would eat such a dish a bit differently by sopping up the filling with the bread. Certain spices like allspice and clove make the experience comforting. However, I urge you to consider other possibilities that offer substance and flavor.

 HEART HEALTH NOTE: Tofu and lentils provide cardiovascular protection via their favorable fatty acids, low glycemic indices, high dietary fiber, folate, and vitamin B12. In addition, studies have demonstrated that lentils and other legumes lower serum homocysteine.

1 medium onion, finely chopped

4 cloves garlic, minced

1 jalapeno, chopped

1 tablespoon Creole Seasoning (see page 247)

½ teaspoon ground allspice

1 cup brown lentils, washed

8 ounces extra-firm tofu, chopped up

1 cup canned San Marzano tomato

½ cup red wine vinegar

1 teaspoon Dijon mustard

½ cup thinly sliced red onion

¼ cup fresh parsley, chopped

½ cup thinly sliced celery

1 cup thinly sliced cabbage (Napa or savoy, if available)

4 whole wheat hamburger buns or sub rolls

Black pepper, as desired

1. In a skillet on medium heat, brown the onions for 5 minutes before adding the garlic.

2. Cook for a minute before adding the spices. Cook for 30 seconds and add the lentils.

3. Stir well and coat the lentils with the onions and spices.

4. Next, add the jalapeno, tofu, tomato, half the vinegar, and just enough water to barely cover the lentils. Season with pepper.

5. Cover the pan and maintain a medium-low heat.

6. The lentils should be cooked in 25 minutes. If the mixture is too wet, strain it and return it to the pan to semi-dry roast for another 10 minutes. Fold in the mustard and parsley. Hold warm.

7. In a bowl, add the remaining vinegar to the cabbage, sliced red onions, and celery.

8. Toast the buns in a skillet or in the oven.

9. Mound the lentil-tofu mixture and top with the cabbage to complete the assembly.

Mushroom Po' Boy

LEVEL 2   SERVINGS: 4

The style of sandwich and its name are said to have originated in the French Quarter district in New Orleans when the Martin Brothers Coffee Stand and Restaurant opened. When the striking streetcar men came for a sandwich, one might have overheard "here comes another poor boy."

HEART HEALTH NOTE: Only in the last few decades have mushroom studies made significant headway. An interesting feature of mushrooms is β-glucans, which are polysaccharides found on the surface of the cell wall. When eaten, our immune systems interact with these β-glucans to stimulate our immune cells. The proposed cardiovascular protective theory supports reduced vascular inflammation via our body's immune response.

4 soft whole wheat sub rolls

12–16 oyster mushrooms (substitute sliced portobello, if unavailable)

¼ cup red wine vinegar

2 tablespoons Creole Seasoning (see page 247), more or less

½ cup garbanzo flour

¼ cup rice flour or corn starch

2 cloves garlic, grated

1 cup Aquafaba (see page 197)

½ teaspoon date syrup

1 teaspoon Dijon mustard

2 tablespoons fresh tarragon, chopped

½ seedless cucumber, diced

2 cups crisp mild lettuce, shredded or sliced thinly

1 large ripe tomato, halved and sliced thinly

Juice and zest of 1 lemon

Water, as needed

Black pepper

1. Dust any dirt off the mushrooms. Transfer them to a bowl, brush them with some red wine vinegar, and toss them in one tablespoon of creole spice.

2. Dust half the garbanzo flour and the rice flour onto the mushrooms along with some pepper. Move the mushrooms around to obtain an even coating.

3. Roast them on a baking sheet at 350°F until golden brown and allow to dry out on a metal rack. Season with more creole blend, as desired.

4. In a bowl, steep the garlic in the lemon juice and zest for 5 minutes. This takes the raw edge off the garlic and may be used immediately. Add the aquafaba, date syrup, mustard, remaining creole blend, cucumber, and tarragon. Mix well and taste this sauce (remoulade). If desired, add some no-sodium hot sauce for an extra kick.

5. The sandwich is assembled easily. Slice the bread lengthwise without separating it. Spread the remoulade generously on both sides. Next, place the lettuce, followed by slices of tomato, and top with the fried mushrooms. Dust with more seasoning or no-sodium hot sauce, as preferred.

Fava Bean Shawarma with Salad

LEVEL 2   SERVINGS: 4

Shawarma are similar to gyros, but the spices make shawarma distinctive. This dish provides all the flavor of a traditional version with the added benefit and contrast of a clean and bright salad.

 HEART HEALTH NOTE: Acetylcholine (ACh) is an endothelial-dependent vaso-dilator. Eggplant contains abundant ACh and can act as an antihypertensive agent while improving vascular perfusion.

4 cloves garlic, smashed

2 tablespoons Bahārāt spice blend (see page 239)

½ teaspoon cinnamon powder

1 red onion, cut into wedges

2 cups fava beans (if unavailable, substitute garbanzo), rehydrated, cooked, and peeled

1 small eggplant, sliced into ¼ inch slices

2 tablespoons red wine vinegar

¼ cup fresh parsley, chopped

1 cup chopped kale

1 cup fresh spinach

1 small seedless cucumber, diced

2 medium ripe tomatoes, diced

Whole wheat pita, cut into small pieces and toasted

Zest and juice of 2 lemons

Black pepper

1. Whisk half the spices, lemon juice and zest, garlic, onions, and pepper in a bowl. Marinate the fava beans and eggplant in this mixture for at least 2 hours.

2. Roast the mixture on a baking sheet in a 350°F oven for 30 minutes. Chop the roasted mixture to a coarse crumb. Towards the last 10 minutes, add the pita pieces to the baking sheet and crisp them.

3. In a bowl, make a dressing with the vinegar, remaining spices, and parsley.

4. Toss the kale in the dressing and massage to soften.

5. Add the spinach, toasted pita, cucumber, and tomato. Toss well and adjust the seasoning, as desired. This is the Fattoush salad.

6. Serve a serving of the fava-eggplant-onion crumb on the Fattoush.

Jumbo Lump Cauliflower Cakes

LEVEL 2   SERVINGS: 4

This is inspired by a jumbo lump crab cake, but frankly, it is more interesting and flavorful.

 HEART HEALTH NOTE: There are seven different types of vegetables found in the lettuce group, including cos (or romaine), butterhead, leaf, stalk (or asparagus), crisphead (or iceberg), Latin, and oilseed. Romaine lettuce is higher in total folate content than spinach which, alongside other B-vitamins, helps break down homocysteine circulating in the blood.

½ large yellow onion, small dice

½ red bell pepper, small dice

½ green bell pepper, small dice

2 sticks celery, small dice

1 cup dry white wine

1 teaspoon minced fresh garlic

2 tablespoons Creole Seasoning (see page 247)

2 cups cooked cauliflower florets (roasted)

2 tablespoons freshly chopped flat-leaf parsley

1 tablespoon Aquafaba (see page 197)

1 teaspoon Dijon mustard

¼ cup chopped fresh tarragon

1 tablespoon flax meal

8 large romaine lettuce leaves, washed and dried

1 tablespoon white balsamic vinegar

¼ cup fresh basil

Juice and zest of 1 lemon

Unseasoned panko breadcrumbs

Black pepper

1. Cook the onions, peppers, and celery in the white wine, until translucent.

2. Add the garlic and creole spice blend. Stir for 30 seconds. Empty contents in a large bowl and let them cool. Add the remaining ingredients except the lemon juice and basil. Fold in the cooked cauliflower carefully, leaving some larger chunks. Slowly add just enough breadcrumbs to be able to form into disks. Do not add too many breadcrumbs and do not pack the disks too tightly. Form into eight cakes.

3. Roast in the oven for 20 minutes, turning once. While the cakes are roasting, grill or roast the romaine lettuce until they brown a bit, and the leaves begin wilting.

4. Chop the grilled romaine into large pieces and mix with the lemon juice plus zest and the basil.

5. Serve two cauliflower cakes with a serving of grilled romaine.

Zucchini Phad Thai

LEVEL 2   **SERVINGS: 4**

Certainly, this recipe can also be made with traditional rice or buckwheat noodles and that would be a good dinner option. Using zucchini noodles makes this a lighter lunch option.

 HEART HEALTH NOTE: Zucchini has high levels of carotenoids, which are natural pigments in food. Oxidative stress acts as a trigger for atherosclerosis. Zucchini has been found to lower oxidative stress in impaired vascular patients by decreasing inflammation and the uptake of carotenoids by enterocyte. Oils rich in long-chain triglycerides were reported to be more effective in solubilizing β-carotene, like soybean or safflower oil.

8 ounces firm tofu, sliced into ½-inch slabs

1 cup Manchurian sauce (see page 228)

1 cup scallions, sliced

1 teaspoon fresh ginger, minced

1 teaspoon fresh garlic, minced

¼ cup rice wine vinegar

4 cups Zucchini noodles (use a spiralizer or equivalent tool)

¼ cup roasted, unsalted peanuts, chopped

1 tablespoon toasted sesame seeds

1 cup fresh cilantro with tender stems

1 cup bean sprouts

Juice and zest of 1 lime

Lime wedges, for additional brightness

1. Marinate the sliced tofu in half the Manchurian sauce for about 15 minutes.

2. Cook the marinated tofu over low heat in a non-stick pan or bake in the oven at 350°F for 30 minutes.

3. In a bowl, make a dressing with the remaining Manchurian sauce, scallions, ginger, garlic, lime juice and zest, and rice wine vinegar.

4. Gently toss the zucchini noodles in the dressing.

5. Assemble a serving of noodles, cooked tofu, sprinkle of chopped peanuts, sesame seeds, fresh cilantro, and bean sprouts. Mix gently.

6. Serve with a lime wedge.

Eggplant Green Curry

LEVEL 2   **SERVINGS: 4**

Anise and eggplant (aka aubergine) have a natural affinity for each other in my opinion. The fragrance and fresh notes of a Thailand-inspired green curry pairs perfectly with the refreshing qualities of fennel. Certainly, one could add a plant-based protein like tofu, but in this case, I think the harmonious interplay between the eggplant soaking up the gravy flavors and the textural contrast offered by the fennel bulb and seeds is a transcendent experience. The addition of soybeans provides adequate nutritious plant-based protein.

 HEART HEALTH NOTE: Fennel bulb is an antioxidant that increases satiety and reduces food intake. Fennel can delay gastrointestinal transit and reduce fat absorption. The exact mechanism of fennel remains unknown but can also improve the lipid profile of a dish.

1 teaspoon fennel seed

2 kaffir lime leaves, sliced very thinly

1 tablespoon fresh ginger, sliced thinly

3 garlic cloves, minced

1 fennel bulb, medium diced, keep the fronds for garnish

3 Japanese eggplant, sliced on a bias into ½-inch slices

1 cup Green Curry Concentrate (see page 208)

½ cup rice wine vinegar

1 cup cooked edamame

2 cups chopped Swiss chard, leaves and stems

1 cup low fat coconut milk, more or less

4 mint leaves, torn

2 sprigs cilantro, chopped

4 basil leaves, torn

2 cups cooked brown rice, unsalted

Water or unsalted vegetable stock, as needed

Juice of 1 lime

Pinch of sugar, more or less

Black pepper

1. Heat a heavy bottomed pot over medium heat and add the fennel seeds and lime leaves.

2. After 15 seconds, add the ginger and garlic. Cook for a minute until the garlic starts browning a bit.

3. Now add the chopped fennel bulb and cook for 5 minutes before adding the eggplant. Stir well and after 10 minutes, add the green curry concentrate and mix well.

4. Add the rice wine vinegar, some water or stock to loosen the sauce a bit. After 5 minutes, add the cooked edamame, Swiss chard leaves and stems, and coconut milk, stirring well. Adjust the sugar and pepper as desired. Simmer on low for 10 minutes.

5. As soon as the eggplant is soft and cooked, turn off the heat, add the lime juice, and fold in all the fresh herbs (mint, cilantro, and basil).

6. Serve with cooked brown rice.

West Indian Curry

This dish is inspired by a commonly available plate through our travels in Jamaica. I have combined culturally appropriate ingredients with foundational flavors that justify the use of the term "West Indian." The flavors are vibrant, spiced, and rich all at the same time.

HEART HEALTH NOTE: Field peas (or cowpeas) can improve hypercholesterolemia, as do many legumes. They can also reduce plasma LDL and add a plant protein source to your diet. A recent study noted total protein intake has a correlation with the reduction of all-cause mortality, but plant-based proteins had a reduction in all-cause *and* cardiovascular mortality.

1 small onion, chopped

1 red or yellow bell pepper, cored and chopped

1 tablespoon fresh ginger, minced

1 tablespoon fresh garlic, minced

½ cup Jerk Seasoning (see page 240)

¼ cup rice wine vinegar

1 pound callaloo greens (leafy green in the amaranth family), substitute collard greens if necessary

2 cups field peas, cooked

2 medium or 1 large, sweet potato, diced

2 cups low fat coconut or oat milk

¼ cup fresh turmeric, minced (substitute dried powder using only 1 teaspoon)

2 tablespoons sugar or date syrup, as needed

2 cups cooked brown rice

Fresh herbs like cilantro or mint, as desired

Water, as needed

1. In a saucepan over medium heat, cook the onions, turmeric, peppers, ginger, and garlic for 5 minutes, stirring to ensure the garlic doesn't burn.

2. Add the jerk blend and vinegar and cook for five minutes before adding the greens and peas. Cover and cook for 10 minutes.

3. Add the sweet potato with enough water to just cover the solids. Simmer covered for 20 minutes or until the greens are just cooked.

4. Add the coconut or oat milk, stir well. Adjust the spice and acidity levels.

5. Serve with cooked brown rice and your favorite fresh herbs.

Roasted Vegetable Tikka Masala Curry

LEVEL 3   SERVINGS: 4

This British interpretation of so much of what they loved about Indian food has now become representative of Indian cuisine the world over. The foundational tikka masala sauce is versatile and balanced making it a great option for a wide variety of quick dishes, once you already have the sauce made from your prep day.

 HEART HEALTH NOTE: In studies, curry leaves were found to help reduce dyslipidemia, arteriosclerosis, and oxidative stress markers when compared to statin groups. Curry leaves can even inhibit platelet aggregation when combined with coriander.

½ inch piece of fresh ginger, minced

2 cloves garlic, minced

4 curry leaves (if available)

1 small onion, chopped

1 small green bell pepper, chopped

2 cups firm tofu, cut into cubes

4 cups of assorted blanched and dry roasted seasonal vegetables, unsalted

3 cups Tikka Masala sauce (see page 212)

¼ cup apple cider vinegar

1 cup oat milk

2 cups cooked brown rice

Water, as needed

Pinch of sugar, more or less

Fresh cilantro for garnish

1. In a saucepan, over medium heat, cook ginger, garlic, and curry leaves for two minutes.

2. Next, add the onions and bell pepper. Cook this for about 5 minutes.

3. Now add the tofu and cook for two minutes before adding the cooked vegetables.

4. Now add the tikka masala sauce and a bit of water to thin it out. Stir everything for a minute or so. Now add the apple cider vinegar, and some sugar.

5. Stir well and simmer on low for two or three minutes. Finish by stirring in the oat milk.

6. Taste the sauce and adjust the seasonings as desired. Serve with the cooked brown rice and a sprinkle of chopped cilantro.

Kofta Creole & Grits

LEVEL 3   SERVINGS: 4

This is my plant-based take on a classic dish from the American South. I thought long and hard about the best way to celebrate the creole sauce, and decided on serving it over grits. The kofta holds up to the strong and comforting flavors.

 HEART HEALTH NOTE: Almonds have been consistently proven to reduce the risk of CVD, ischemic heart disease and may not only offer protection against heart disease but also increase longevity. Almonds also improve blood pressure, flow-mediated dilatation and antioxidant defenses with polyphenols, PUFA fats, flavonoids, L-arginine and fiber.

8 ounces extra-firm tofu

1 shallot, minced

½ inch piece fresh ginger, minced

2 cloves of garlic, roughly chopped

1 any type of medium-hot green chili, minced

1 teaspoon Creole Seasoning (see page 247)

2 cups Creole Marinade (see page 206)

1 small potato, boiled

1 cup coarse ground yellow corn grits

¼ cup almonds, toasted and ground

¼ cup fresh parsley, chopped

1 cup diced shiitake mushrooms

1 shallot or small red onion, minced

2 tablespoons fresh thyme, chopped

2 cups dry white wine

2 cups oat milk

Water as needed (approximately 4 cups total)

Unsalted breadcrumbs, as needed

Black pepper, as needed

1. Chop up the tofu into medium sized pieces and roast on a baking sheet in a 350°F oven for 20 minutes.

2. While the tofu is roasting, roast the shallot, ginger, and garlic in a pan. After a couple of minutes, add the green chili and creole spice blend. Cook for a few seconds before adding the cooked potato. Smash it into the mixture and transfer all the ingredients to a bowl to cool down.

3. After the tofu comes out of the oven and cools a bit, add it to the same bowl along with the ground almonds and chopped parsley. Mix well. Taste the mixture and season with pepper, and perhaps more creole spices, as desired. Add just enough breadcrumbs to be able to form 12 balls. Bake them in an oven for 15 minutes until lightly golden brown.

4. In a heavy-bottomed pan, cook the mushrooms and shallot for 3 minutes. Add both cups of white wine and cook for 1 minute. Add two cups of water and one cup of oat milk. Bring to a low simmer and start whisking in the grits. Keep stirring until you notice that the grits start getting thick. Turn down the heat to medium-low and cook the grits for 45 minutes or until they are soft, adding more water if it's too thick or dry. Stirring periodically will ensure creamier grits and one without lumps.

5. Warm the creole sauce for about 10 minutes. Taste and finish with 1 cup of oat milk.

6. Serve the dish with grits on the bottom, then some creole sauce, and three browned koftas on top of the sauce. Garnish with chopped parsley.

Mushroom & Leafy Greens Burger

LEVEL 2   **SERVINGS: 2**

By changing the ingredients of the burger, it is possible to attain a wide variety of flavors and textures.

 HEART HEALTH NOTE: Edible mushrooms appear to improve cardio-metabolic disease. Current experimental research suggests daily mushroom consumption may improve fasting blood glucose, C-reactive protein, and triglycerides. However, few studies have been devoted to their consumption and assessment of CVD.

1 pound assorted
   mushrooms, diced
4 ounce firm tofu, cubed
1 large red onion, small diced
2 tablespoons fresh garlic, minced
2 cups kale, chopped finely
4 cups cooking spinach (heat in
   a pan to wilt)
2 cups arugula
2 tablespoons Tuscan Spice Blend
   (see page 243)

2 tablespoons fresh flat-leaf
   parsley, chopped
¼ cup flax seed soaked in
   warm water
¼ cup red wine vinegar
   (more, if preferred)
Panko breadcrumbs, as needed
Black pepper, as needed
Whole wheat or whole grain
   hamburger buns
Preferred burger toppings
   (no-sodium and fat-free)

1. Preheat oven to 350°F and, on a baking sheet, roast the mushrooms and tofu, seasoned a bit with the Tuscan spice blend for 30 minutes.

2. After all ingredients have cooled, mix all the ingredients except the breadcrumbs, in a large bowl. Add enough breadcrumbs to be able to form about four ½-inch-thick patties. If you are able to make more, store in the fridge for another day or freeze.

3. To finish, toast the patties on a baking sheet in the oven, or in a pan, until golden brown on both sides.

4. Top with a cheese alternative (see pages 199–201), if preferred, and assemble your burgers with the no-sodium, fat-free, plant-based accompaniments that you prefer. It will be enjoyable to dress the lettuce or greens with red wine vinegar.

Dinner

DINNER IS OFTEN THE most relaxed meal of the day, offering a chance to appreciate and savor each bite. It is essential that dinner complements the flavors, inspiration, and nutrition of your other meals. This section features recipes designed to enhance your enjoyment during preparation and reinforce the art of dining. These comforting and exciting dishes draw inspiration from a variety of cuisines, promising a delightful culinary experience.

Loaded Roasted Sweet Potato

LEVEL 1   **SERVINGS: 4**

A loaded baked (usually, russet) potato is a familiar canvas, but when that tuber is a sweet potato, suddenly, the natural sweetness, creaminess, and health benefits offer an entirely different and better gastronomic experience.

 HEART HEALTH NOTE: Sweet potatoes are high in flavonoids like quercetin, ranging from moderate to high as their colors intensifies, with yellow being the lowest and purple the highest. Their tannins reduce serum creatinine and lactate-dehydrogenase activity, favoring cardiovascular health. Additionally, the antho-cyanins found in plant pigments are endothelially protective, decreasing blood pressure and platelet formation while increasing HDL.

4 medium sweet potatoes

1 small onion, chopped

1 12-ounce can black beans, no-sodium, drained and rinsed

¼ cup apple cider vinegar

1 large fresh tomato

2 ripe avocados

¼ cup roasted, unsalted pepitas (pumpkin seeds) or almonds

½ cup scallions, sliced thinly

1 jalapeno, chopped (optional)

1 lime, juice and zest

¼ cup fresh cilantro, chopped

Black pepper

1. Place the sweet potatoes on a baking sheet and roast in the oven at 350°F for 45 minutes (maybe less), until soft.

2. In a bowl, mix the onion, beans, vinegar, tomato, scallions, jalapeno, lime juice and zest and cilantro. Taste and adjust the acidity and spice per your preference.

3. Make a pocket in the baked sweet potato, fill with the bean mixture, spread cubes of avocado (about half avocado per serving), and sprinkle with the nuts.

West African Inspired Nuts & Greens Stew

LEVEL 1   SERVINGS: 4

This stew exemplifies why so much of the food in the Caribbean and the Southern United States can be traced back to African roots. The spices perfectly complement the earthiness of the greens and the decadence offered by the nuts.

 HEART HEALTH NOTE: The polyphenols found in Habanero peppers highly contribute to their antioxidant activity. When harvested earlier, the polyphenols (found in the flesh of the pepper) further decrease oxidative stress. During this time, the catechin's antioxidant qualities are also at their peak. Later on, gallic acid increases, which are the polyphenols found in the skin of the pepper.

6 cups collard greens, chopped

3 cups spinach

1 medium onion, chopped

4 cloves garlic, minced

1-inch piece fresh ginger, grated or minced

½ habanero pepper, chopped (optional) (substitute ½ teaspoon cayenne pepper)

1 teaspoon ground cumin

1 medium sweet potato, chopped

2 tablespoons tomato paste

¼ cup ground walnuts

1 tablespoon no-sodium peanut butter

¼ cup toasted unsalted peanuts

2 lemons, zest and juice

Water or vegetable broth (no-sodium), as needed

Black pepper, as desired

1. In a pot, roast the onion, garlic, and ginger for 5 minutes.

2. Add the tomato paste and cook for a minute.

3. Add the greens and spices and cook for 5 minutes.

4. Now add the sweet potato, ground walnuts, peanut butter, and stock or water to cover the ingredients in the pot by about one inch. Mix well.

5. Cover and simmer on medium-low for 20 minutes. Taste the stew and adjust the acidity and spice as desired.

6. Finish by adding the toasted peanuts, lemon juice and zest. Serve with cooked brown rice or whole grain bread.

Vegetable & Brown Rice Paella

LEVEL 2   SERVINGS: 4

They tell me it's about the socarrat (the crisp and caramelized bottom layer), but there's so much more. The timing of adding ingredients has a lot to do with the outcome. Be sure to have enough warm broth on hand should the rate of evaporation be faster than expected. Also, allow the finished dish to rest and absorb every last bit of the broth for the perfect paella.

 HEART HEALTH NOTE: Brown rice is an ancient grain, but its nutritional impact can be elevated with germination. Germinated brown rice is high in natural gamma-aminobutyric acid (GABA), which can play a role in reducing blood pressure and protecting cardiovascular function.

2 cups sliced cremini mushrooms

4 cloves garlic, sliced thinly

1 red bell pepper, cored and sliced

1 green pepper, cored and sliced

1 orange or yellow pepper, cored and sliced

2 red onions, sliced

3 tablespoons tomato paste

1 tablespoon smoked paprika

2 cups brown rice, washed and rinsed

2 cups fresh greens like mustard greens or kale

2 cups dry white wine

2 quarts of warm, unsalted vegetable stock, more as needed

Chopped parsley, as needed for garnish

1. Use a flat sauté pan or a proper paella pan for this dish. Over medium-high heat, cook the mushrooms in the wine for a couple of minutes.

2. Next, add the garlic, peppers, and onions and cook on medium heat for 5 minutes.

3. Next, add the tomato paste and cook for 2 minutes before adding the smoked paprika, rice, and greens.

4. Stir well and even out the rice and other ingredients in the pan.

5. Add the warm stock one ladle at a time, but do not disturb the rice. Cook for at least 45 minutes or until the rice is cooked and a crust has formed on the bottom. You may partially cover the rice for the first 30 minutes to ensure the brown rice cooks through.

6. Allow the rice to rest for at least 10 minutes to absorb all the broth.

7. Finish by sprinkling parsley on the cooked rice. Be sure to serve the socarrat with every portion.

Brown Rice Stuffed Pepper

LEVEL 1   SERVINGS: **4**

This was a surprise dinner one night and I knew right away that it was going to make its way into a cookbook one day. I cannot think of a better forum than here.

 HEART HEALTH NOTE: *Capsicum annuum* encompasses a wide variety of shapes and sizes of peppers, including sweet bell peppers, a few chili peppers, New Mexico chili and cayenne peppers. All have antioxidant and anti-inflammatory activities beneficial in the prevention of cardiovascular disease.

4 large yellow or red bell peppers, cored

2 cups brown rice, cooked

1 shallot or small red onion, minced

1 cup kale, chopped finely

1 jalapeno, chopped finely (optional, use as much as you desire)

2 sticks celery, chopped finely

1 tablespoon freshly chopped parsley leaves

¼ cup Macadamia nuts or almonds, chopped coarsely

¼ cup apple cider vinegar

1 lemon, zest and juice

Black pepper, as desired

1. Cut across the pepper at the stem end and carefully scoop out the seeds and excess pulp. This constitutes the cap of the finished dish. Retain the stem of the cap for a nicer presentation.

2. In a bowl, mix the brown rice, shallot, celery, kale, Jalapeno, parsley, nuts, vinegar, lemon juice and zest, and black pepper. Essentially, this is a brown rice salad. Taste it and adjust acidity and other flavors.

3. Fill each hollowed out pepper with the brown rice salad.

4. Place the stuffed peppers on a baking sheet, replace the cap, and roast in the oven at 350°F for 45 minutes. Allow the roasted peppers to cool a bit.

5. Serve as is or with a side salad.

Farro Risotto

LEVEL 1   **SERVINGS: 4**

Risotto is a popular Italian rice-based dish. By using an ancient Roman grain like farro, one achieves a heartier, tastier, and more cook-friendly version of risotto because farro holds up well to cooking, unlike rice. After you make this recipe once, it will become apparent that other versions keeping farro a constant will come naturally.

HEART HEALTH NOTE: Whole grains can have a beneficial effect on a person's risk of cardiovascular disease. Ancient grains, like farro, are technically pseudocereals, meaning they are gluten-free and have been shown to improve elevated inflammatory markers (CRP), blood pressure and blood lipids found in coronary and cardiovascular disease.

½ cup farro

½ cup wild rice

½ cup pearl barley

1 shallot or small red onion, minced

1 teaspoon minced fresh garlic

3 cups Swiss chard, leaves and stems, chopped

2 cups dry white wine

4 cups vegetable stock (no-sodium) or water, or more

1 lemon, juice, and zest

½ cup toasted almonds

Black pepper, as desired

1. In a saucepan, toast the farro, wild rice, and barley on medium heat for 5 minutes.

2. Add the onion, garlic, and Swiss chard and cook for another 5 minutes.

3. Add the white wine and some black pepper. Cook for 2 minutes.

4. Add the stock or water and bring to a simmer.

5. Without covering and stirring periodically, cook the mixture on a steady simmer. Add more liquid if it starts to dry up too much. After about 40 minutes, barley and farro should be cooked.

6. Finish by mixing in the lemon juice and lemon zest and sprinkling on some toasted almonds.

Quinoa Primavera

LEVEL 1   SERVINGS: 4

Pasta primavera is every vegetarian's nemesis in restaurants because, aside from a plate of sides and the predictable pasta primavera, even many professional cooks seem to struggle with being creative. Quinoa replacing pasta makes this an entirely more healthful and interesting dish. It's also very easy to put together, especially if you already have some cooked quinoa from prep day.

HEART HEALTH NOTE: The combination of different mechanisms can create better cardiac benefits than either component provides independently. Barley is high in insoluble fiber, which helps support a cardioprotective gut biome and reduces LDL cholesterol. Wild rice improves flow-mediated dilation of arteriole smooth muscle in adults with mild endothelial dysfunction.

2 cups water

1 cup dry white wine

1 bay leaf

1 cup white quinoa, washed well and rubbed under water to soften the hull

2 shallots or 1 medium red onion, sliced thinly

2 lemons, zest and juice

2 cloves garlic, sliced thinly

1 medium ripe tomato, chopped

1 red bell pepper, cored and chopped

1 yellow bell pepper, cored and chopped

2 cups frozen peas

2 tablespoons fresh thyme leaves, chopped coarsely

2 cups fresh spinach

Black pepper, to taste

1. Bring the water, ½ cup wine, bay leaf, and some black pepper to a simmer. Add the quinoa, stir well, cover, and cook on low for 20 minutes until you see the white sprouts indicating that the quinoa is cooked. Keep covered for 15 minutes.

2. In a saucepan over medium heat, heat the remaining wine, shallots, lemon juice and zest, garlic, and tomatoes.

3. Add the peppers, peas, thyme, and some black pepper.

4. As soon as the peas are warmed through and the peppers are soft, add the cooked quinoa and spinach. The heat of the dish should wilt the spinach.

Bucatini Fra Diavolo

LEVEL 1   **SERVINGS: 4**

Brother Devil (fra diavolo) sounds sinful, but there's nothing errant about a spicy pasta dish. I don't know if Marcela Hazan would have approved of transforming her perfect sauce in this manner, but I've meant as an homage to the versatility of her sauce. The bucatini noodle is interesting enough with the hole through the center, but a bright and spicy sauce with the usual herbaceous and aromatic accents makes this a thoroughly enjoyable Roman-style pasta dish.

 HEART HEALTH NOTE: Vinegar is a unique compound produced via the complex fermentation of grain or fruits. Tetramethylpyrazine (TMP), which naturally exists in fermented foods, provides protection to the heart muscle cells and aids in repairing blood vessel injuries.

6 garlic cloves, minced

1 teaspoon Calabrian chiles (or other spicy red pepper), chopped

1 teaspoon red chili flakes, more or less

2 shallots, minced

1 stalk celery, small diced

1 cup dry white wine

¼ cup white balsamic vinegar

2 cups canned San Marzano tomatoes with juices (no salt version)

1 pound whole wheat bucatini, dried

¼ cup finely chopped basil

¼ cup finely chopped flat-leaf parsley

½ cup oat milk

Black pepper

1. First, we will make the base sauce. In a pan, cook the garlic on medium heat until it browns slightly.

2. Add the chili flakes and Calabrian chiles. Cook for a few seconds before adding the shallots and celery. Cook for 5 minutes and add the white wine and vinegar. After two minutes, add the tomatoes and simmer for 20 minutes. Blend the sauce to a smooth consistency. Hold it warm.

3. Cook the pasta in boiling water and, a minute away from being al dente, ladle some pasta water into the tomato sauce. Drain the pasta well and add it to the sauce. Maintain a medium-low temperature to continue cooking the paste to the al dente stage or the desired doneness.

4. Be sure to gently mix the pasta around so it cooks evenly and doesn't stick to the pan. Taste the sauce and pasta one more time before finishing with the fresh herbs and oat milk.

5. Note that this dish should be spicy, so there is a lot of variability as to exactly how spicy one desires. Serve with some garlic rubbed grilled or oven roasted bread.

Pasta alla Norma

Eggplant, tomato, garlic, olive oil, chiles...what's not to like? For my money, this Catanian (Sicily) staple beats an eggplant parmigiana for its focused and mature flavors any day and all day. The pasta can be left out altogether and what remains is a testament to the world-wide popularity of Italian cuisine.

 HEART HEALTH NOTE: Eggplants have many cardiovascular properties. One example is the compound delphinidin, which can induce endothelial vasodilation by the activation of the nitric oxide (NO) pathway. Delphinidin also reduces the angiotensin-converting enzyme ACE. Another benefit can be found in eggplant's chlorogenic acid, which enhances the NO pathway, therefore improving endothelial function and lowering blood pressure.

2 medium Italian eggplants, chopped

1 sprig fresh thyme

4 cloves garlic, sliced thinly

1 bell pepper, cored and chopped

2 cups dry white wine

½ teaspoon crushed red pepper flakes or Calabrian chili (more or less)

2 cups canned San Marzano tomatoes with juices (no salt version)

1 pound whole wheat penne or rotini pasta

¼ cup chopped almonds

½ cup fresh basil leaves, coarse chopped without bruising

Black pepper, as desired

1. Wash the eggplant and cut them into ¾-inch pieces. Toss in some pepper and the sprig of thyme. Roast in a 375°F degree oven for about 30 minutes. Turn over the eggplant once during the roasting process.

2. In a wide pan, brown the garlic and bell pepper on medium heat before adding wine and the crushed pepper. Cook for a minute before adding the tomatoes. Cook for 15 minutes.

3. Add the roasted eggplant. Taste the sauce, adjust the acidity and spice. Hold warm.

4. Cook the pasta in boiling water and, a minute away from being al dente, ladle some pasta water into the eggplant and tomato sauce. Drain the pasta well and add it to the sauce. Maintain a medium-low temperature to continue cooking the paste to the al dente stage or the desired doneness.

5. Finish with fresh basil and almonds.

Brown Rice & Red Lentil Khichadi

LEVEL 1   **SERVINGS: 4**

This is a humble one-pot meal enjoyed all over the Indian subcontinent. It is extremely nutritious and keeps well. In fact, it is common to feed babies *Khichadi* for their first solid food.

HEART HEALTH NOTE: Mushrooms produce a compound called ergothioneine which decreases pro-inflammatory adhesion molecules during atherogenesis. They also work as prebiotics in our intestinal microflora's fermentation, inhibiting HMG-CoA reductase and thereby slowing cholesterol production.

1 small onion, diced

½ cup carrots, diced

2 cups assorted mushrooms, coarse chopped

1-inch piece ginger, minced

1 bay leaf

2 green chilies or 1 jalapeño, minced

1 cup red lentils, washed and drained

1 cup brown rice

1 teaspoon turmeric powder

¼ cup edamame or green peas

1 cup apple cider vinegar

4 cups vegetable stock or water

1. In a shallow pot with a proper lid, roast the onions, carrots, ginger, bay leaf, mushrooms, and chilies on medium heat for about 5 minutes.

2. Next, add the lentils, brown rice, and turmeric powder. Cook for about 15 minutes, stirring frequently.

3. Now add the edamame or peas, stir well, and add the vinegar and water. Stir well and taste the broth to make sure its acidity is to your liking.

4. Cover the pot, reduce the heat to low-medium and cook for 20 minutes.

5. Serve with your favorite fresh herbs and perhaps, some non-dairy, fat free yogurt.

Mung Bean & Turmeric Bowl

LEVEL 1   **SERVINGS: 4**

Mung beans are extremely nutritious, as is turmeric. So, on paper, this might seem like nutrition for the sake of nutrition. However, there's a reason turmeric appears in so many Indian dishes. It provides an earthy umami that is uniquely deep.

HEART HEALTH NOTE: Mung beans provide a protein dose-dependent reduction in plasma lipids levels, triglyceride (TG) and HDL. The mechanism for mung bean's cholesterol-lowering activity is speculated to come from an increase in GI acids and plant sterol excretion.

½ teaspoon cumin seed

½-inch piece fresh ginger, minced

1-inch piece fresh turmeric, sliced thinly (substitute 1 teaspoon turmeric powder)

1 shallot, sliced thinly

1 green chili, minced (optional)

1 cup cooked, sprouted, or rehydrated mung beans, cooked in water and a teaspoon of turmeric

¼ cup roasted peanuts, unsalted

2 cups fresh kale, washed dried, and chopped

¼ cup red wine vinegar

Zest and juice of 1 lemon or lime

Black pepper, as desired

1. In a pot over medium heat, add the cumin seed, ginger, and fresh turmeric. After a minute, add the shallot and green chili and cook for another minute or two.

2. Next, add the cooked mung beans and peanuts. Stir the mixture and heat for a couple of minutes.

3. Season with pepper, as preferred, and cool a bit but not completely. Add the zest and juice of the lime and vinegar to the kale and massage with a touch of pepper. Finally, mix the kale with the mung bean mixture (while still slightly warm) and let sit for 5 minutes before serving.

Broccoli & White Bean Casserole

LEVEL 2   **SERVINGS: 4**

I saved this familiar dish for towards the end of the book. For no other reason other than to encourage you to use the vast experience you would have gained by this stage in your progression through the book. Doing so may very well help you prepare one of the best casseroles you may have ever had.

 HEART HEALTH NOTE: Cloves are the unopened flower bud of the clove tree and is originally native to Indonesia. Cloves have antioxidant and anti-inflammatory capacities that plays a cardiovascular role, along with being touted as significantly lowering cholesterol. While generally recognized as safe (GRAS), further cardiovascular research is needed to support this position in healthcare.

½ cup oat milk
1 cup cashew nuts
1 tablespoon nutritional yeast
4 garlic cloves, minced
2 slices multi-grain, low-sodium bread
2 medium yellow onions, chopped
¼ cup tomato paste

2 medium heads broccoli (about 2 pounds), cut into small, bite-sized florets
2 tablespoons red wine vinegar
1 cup water or vegetable stock (no-sodium)
2 cans cannellini beans (no-sodium), drained, rinsed
Juice and zest of 1 lemon
Black pepper, as desired

1. Warm the oat milk and soak the cashews, the nutritional yeast, 1 clove of garlic, and lemon zest for 15 minutes. Blend to a thick sauce.

2. Toast the bread, allow it to cool and pulse in a food processor to form breadcrumbs.

3. Cook the onions, tomato paste, lemon juice, broccoli, vinegar, and water until the broccoli is cooked.

4. In a baking pan, first layer some breadcrumbs, then the broccoli mixture, then beans, followed by the cashew sauce.

5. Bake uncovered in a 350°F oven for 30 minutes.

6. Allow the casserole to cool before serving with perhaps a salad.

Heart-Healthy Bolognese

LEVEL 2   **SERVINGS: 4**

In my view, a traditional Bolognese is as defined as it is vague. Without a pasta or polenta, Bolognese is just chili—not that there's anything wrong with that. This dish is as wildly comforting as it is tasty.

 HEART HEALTH NOTE: Cornmeal (also known as maize) is an ancient grain which originated in the Americas. It helps cultivate a cardioprotective gut biome by reducing TMAO and lowering LDL cholesterol.

1 large onion, minced

2 small carrots, small dice

2 stalks celery, small dice

1 bay leaf

5 cloves garlic, sliced thinly

1 sprig rosemary leaves, chopped

2 sprigs fresh thyme leaves, chopped

2 cups dry white wine

1 cup firm tofu

2 cups brown lentils

2 cups canned San Marzano tomatoes, no-sodium

2 cups oat milk

½ teaspoon freshly grated nutmeg

2 cups assorted mushrooms, diced

1 cup dry fine cornmeal (polenta)

3 cups water, more or less

Black pepper

1. In a heavy-bottomed pan, heat the onions, carrots, and celery until they start browning and sweating a bit. Cook for 5 minutes before adding the fresh herbs, bay leaf, and garlic.

2. Cook for an additional 5 minutes and add 1 cup of wine. Cook the mixture for 5 minutes before adding the tofu, lentils, and tomatoes. Season with some pepper and simmer on medium-low.

3. Cook this sauce for another 30 minutes before adding the oat milk and freshly grated nutmeg. Stir and cook for 45 minutes, stirring occasionally. The sauce should be thick and creamy.

4. Cook the mushrooms in the remaining white wine and 2 cups water. Slowly whisk in the cornmeal and cook the polenta according to the package directions. Quick cooking polenta cooks in 5–10 minutes.

5. Ladle a serving of polenta making a small well in the center. Add a serving of lentil sauce, and finish with some chopped fresh parsley.

Cannellini Cassoulet

LEVEL 2   SERVINGS: 4

Cassoulet is a slow-cooked casserole-style stew containing various proteins and white beans. A popular dish that is said to have originated in the Languedoc region of southwest France was historically a rustic and homey dish. Now, one may find renditions in the finest restaurants. I think the assorted mushrooms and potato are a more than adequate replacement for traditional proteins.

 HEART HEALTH NOTE: Turnips have high nitrate levels and enhances the dietary NO pathway. As a cruciferous plant, turnip greens pack even more of a nitrate boost.

1 large onion, medium diced

2 small carrots, medium diced

2 stalks celery, medium diced

4 cloves garlic, sliced thinly

1 tablespoon tomato paste

1 Yukon gold potato, large chunks

1 turnip, large chunks

1 tablespoon Herbs de Provence spice blend (see page 246)

2 cups dry white wine

¼ cup white balsamic vinegar

1 Classic Bouquet Garni (see page 196)

1 medium ripe tomato, small diced

2 small cans or 1 large can cannellini beans, no-sodium, drained and rinsed

Water or vegetable stock, as needed

Fresh parsley for garnish (optional)

Whole wheat bread as accompaniment (optional)

Black pepper, as desired

1. In a heavy-bottomed pot on medium heat, roast the onions, carrots, and celery for about 5 minutes.

2. Next, add the garlic and cook for another 2 minutes before adding the tomato paste. Roast for another 5 minutes, stirring periodically.

3. Now add the potato and turnip and mix gently. Add the spice blend and roast for a few seconds.

4. Add the white wine and vinegar and cook for 2 minutes.

5. Next, add the *bouquet garni*, fresh tomatoes, beans, and enough stock or water to just cover the contents of the pot. Scrape the bottom of the pot to release the flavor into the stew.

6. Cover the pot and cook on low for 15 minutes.

7. If desired, garnish each serving with fresh parsley and serve with crusty whole wheat bread or toast.

Cauliflower & Broccoli Tajine

LEVEL 2   SERVINGS: 4

A few years ago, we wandered about and lost ourselves in the maze that is Old Marrakech. Many a tajine was consumed, but the most memorable version was home-cooked by our Riad manager. She created the most beautiful vegetable version with a garnish of caramelized onions and raisins. And the fluffiest couscous I've ever had. This version is inspired by that memory.

 HEART HEALTH NOTE: Cauliflower and broccoli are particularly heart-healthy choices to include in tajine cooking originating from North Africa. They are high in fiber and loaded with antioxidants helping reduce blood pressure and inflammation. Onions are quercetin-rich, which increases NO and endothelial function. Onions also contain antioxidants that fight cardiac and cancer inflammation, decrease triglycerides, and reduce cholesterol levels.

3 cups cauliflower florets

3 cups broccoli florets

1 sweet potato, peeled and large diced

1 medium onion, peeled, sliced

1 tablespoon fresh ginger, minced

4 cloves garlic, peeled, and sliced into slivers

Pinch of saffron threads, soaked in warm water

1 tablespoon cumin powder

1 teaspoon coriander powder

½ teaspoon cinnamon powder

2 lemons, de-seeded and quartered

2 cups unsalted vegetable stock

½ cup chopped parsley

½ cup chopped cilantro

2 bay leaves

Unsalted vegetable stock, as needed

1. Preheat the oven to 325°F.

2. Heat a tajine, Dutch oven, or shallow pot on medium heat and sear the cauliflower and broccoli in two stages and set aside.

3. Roast the sweet potato and onions until browned. Add the lemon wedges, ginger, garlic, and ground spices. Stir for a minute or so.

4. Add the cauliflower and broccoli back to the pot and deglaze with enough vegetable stock to barely cover the squash and add the saffron threads with the soaking liquid.

5. Test the seasoning, adding more spices as desired.

6. Cover tightly and bake in the oven for about 20 minutes.

7. Remove from the oven and let the tajine rest for about 15 minutes before sprinkling with the chopped parsley and cilantro.

8. Serve with fluffy couscous.

Mushroom Stroganoff

LEVEL 2   SERVINGS: **4**

Stroganoff may be one of the most popular mushroom-based sauces over noodles ever created. This recipe follows the integrity of a classic stroganoff while keeping the recipe plant-based. By serving the stroganoff over mashed turnips and simply cooked green beans, you will find the outcome to be comforting and elegant all at once.

HEART HEALTH NOTE: Aside from its nitrate boosting abilities, turnip bulbs and turnip greens are high in both fiber and water content. Turnips contain choline; higher intake levels of free choline (FC) have been associated with a lower risk of CVD.

1 tablespoon cornstarch

2 cups oat milk

2 tablespoons Dijon mustard

2 tablespoons nutritional yeast

4 medium turnips, washed and quartered

¼ cup fresh parsley, chopped

1 medium onion

4 cloves garlic, minced

3 cups assorted mushrooms (button, cremini, shiitake with stems removed, etc.)

2 cups dry white wine

¼ cup white balsamic vinegar

2 cups sodium and fat free vegetable broth

1 tablespoon onion powder

1 teaspoon garlic powder

½ teaspoon smoked paprika

20 green beans, washed, ends nipped

2 tablespoons red wine vinegar

1 tablespoon fresh thyme

Water, as needed

Black pepper, as desired

1. In a saucepan, heat the cornstarch, 1 cup oat milk, mustard, nutritional yeast, some water, and some black pepper. Keep whisking until the sauce thickens a bit. Hold warm.

2. In a pan, boil the turnips in water until soft, drain well, add some oat milk and smash until the texture is somewhat smooth. Add half the parsley and mix well. Hold warm.

3. In a pan, roast the onions and garlic until golden brown, add the mushrooms and continue cooking on medium-high heat as the mushrooms begin to release their moisture. Continue cooking for 10 minutes before adding the wine, thyme, and white balsamic vinegar. Cook for 2 minutes before adding the oat milk sauce, onion powder, garlic powder, and smoked paprika. Cook for 5 minutes or until the mushrooms have a thick consistency.

4. Cook the green beans in water for 3 minutes, before draining and tossing in the red wine vinegar and black pepper.

5. Serve the mushroom mixture over the mashed turnips accompanied with 5 green beans for a comforting and hearty meal.

Vegetable Paella

They tell me it's about the *socarrat* (the crisp and caramelized bottom layer), but there's so much more. The timing of adding ingredients has a lot to do with the outcome. Be sure to have enough warm seasoned broth on hand should the rate of evaporation be faster than expected. Also, allow the finished dish to rest and absorb every bit of the broth for the perfect paella.

 HEART HEALTH NOTE: Tomato paste affects flow-mediated dilatation. In studies, consumption of tomato paste has been shown to increase the brachial artery diameter via relaxation of the endothelium smooth muscle in the vessel walls, leading to a reduction in diastolic blood pressure (BP).

2 cups sliced cremini mushrooms

1 can garbanzo beans, no-sodium, drained and rinsed well

5 cloves garlic, sliced

2 red bell peppers, cored and sliced

2 cups broccoli florets

2 cups cauliflower florets

2 red onions, sliced

2 tablespoons tomato paste

2 cups arborio or sushi rice

2 cups fresh greens like mustard greens or kale, chopped

2 cups white wine

4 cups or more of warm, unsalted vegetable stock

½ cup sherry vinegar

1 teaspoon smoked paprika

½ cup Spanish olives, rInsed and poached in water for 30 minutes to extract salt

Chopped flat-leaf parsley, as needed for garnish

Pinch of saffron soaked in some warm water

Black pepper, as desired

1. Use a flat heavy-bottomed pan or a proper paella pan for this dish.

2. Over medium-high heat, roast the mushrooms and garbanzo beans for 10 minutes.

3. Next, add the garlic, peppers, broccoli, cauliflower, and onions and cook for 5 minutes.

4. Lower the heat to medium, before adding the tomato paste and smoked paprika. Roast for 2 minutes before adding the rice and greens.

5. Stir well and even out the rice and other ingredients in the pan. Add the white wine, vinegar, and saffron water and cook for about a minute.

6. Now add the warm stock one ladle at a time, but do not disturb the rice. Cook for at least 25 minutes or until the rice is cooked and a crust (socarrat) has formed on the bottom.

7. Let the rice rest for at least 10 minutes to absorb all the broth. Finish by sprinkling the (de-salted) olives and parsley on the cooked rice. Be sure to serve the socarrat with every portion.

Spiced Garbanzo with Brown Rice

LEVEL 2   SERVINGS: 4

Garbanzos cooked in this style also go by the name *Chole* or *Chana Masala* in Indian cuisine. By serving the dish with brown rice and bright garnishes, we are able to achieve a complete meal.

 HEART HEALTH NOTE: Fennel seeds influence the nitrite portion of the dietary NO pathway of vascular functions. Most vegetables of this sort, previously discussed, begin the process from a nitrate point. To provide a quick pathway refresher: nitrate (NO3-) → nitrite (NO2-) → nitric oxide (NO). The end result is increased perfusion and vasorelaxation.

1 teaspoon fennel seeds

1 tablespoon Garam Masala (see page 236)

2 medium sized onions, finely chopped

1-inch ginger, half minced, the other half sliced thinly for garnish

3 garlic cloves, minced

2–3 green chilies, minced

1½ teaspoon turmeric powder

½ teaspoon cayenne pepper

1 tablespoon tomato paste

2 medium-sized tomatoes, finely chopped

2 medium cans of garbanzo beans, drained and rinsed

¼ cup fresh cilantro, chopped

1 cup brown rice, rinsed once

3 cups water or the no-sodium vegetable stock

1 cup dry white wine

Wedges of lime or lemon

1. In a dry skillet, gently toast the fennel seeds, garam masala spice for 5 minutes or until you can sense the aroma of the toasting spices.

2. In a heavy-bottomed saucepan, brown the onions. Add the minced ginger, garlic, and green chilies, and cook for a minute.

3. Next, add ½ teaspoon ground turmeric and cayenne pepper. Cook for one minute, stirring frequently.

4. Add the tomato paste and tomatoes. Stew this spiced mixture for 5 minutes until the tomatoes break down.

5. Now add the garbanzo beans and enough water to just cover. Cover and stew on a medium-low heat for 30 minutes, stirring periodically. Garnish with chopped cilantro, sliced fresh ginger and wedges of lime or lemon.

6. For the rice, read the directions on the package. Usually, it is a two parts water and one part rice ratio.

7. Cook the rice in a mixture of water, 1 teaspoon of turmeric, and wine following the directions.

Red Bean Jambalaya

LEVEL 2   SERVINGS: 4

Traditionally, jambalaya is a creole dish with Spanish and French influences having roots in West African *Joloff*. Every time I visit New Orleans, I make it a point to seek out a good gumbo and jambalaya. And while I have had mixed success with getting what I like, there is no denying the soul of this dish. The mark of a great jambalaya is the balance of spices and the degree to which the rice absorbs the flavor of the broth and aromatics.

 HEART HEALTH NOTE: Eggplant is rich in dietary fiber, which acts to bind lipids and cholesterol, decrease intestinal absorption and increase the fecal excretion of these substances. Also, it can reduce serum cholesterol concentration by inhibiting HMG-CoA reductase activity, the enzyme in cholesterol production.

2 cups eggplant, medium dice

2 cups onions, chopped

1 cup green bell pepper, chopped

1 cup celery, small dice

5 cloves garlic, minced

2 tablespoons smoked or plain paprika

1 teaspoon cayenne pepper

1 tablespoon Creole Seasoning (see page 247)

2 cups brown rice, washed and soaked in water

2 small cans red beans (no-sodium), drained and rinsed well

1 cup tomatoes, diced

½ cup white balsamic vinegar

1 cup carrots, chopped

2 quarts no-sodium vegetable stock, made from all the trims

1 Classic Bouquet Garni (see page 196)

1 bunch flat-leaf parsley, chopped finely

4 lemon wedges

Black pepper, as desired

1. In a wide, heavy-bottomed pot, roast the eggplant and brown.

2. Add the onions, carrots, peppers, and celery to the pot. Roast for a few minutes before adding the garlic, paprika, cayenne, and Creole spice. Stir well.

3. Add the rice and stir to coat each grain well.

4. Return the eggplant to the pot, add the beans and tomatoes, and cook for a couple of minutes.

5. Add the vinegar and enough water or stock based on the amount of rice.

6. Add the bouquet garni, cover the pot and cook the rice starting on medium and returning to low, once it starts simmering. In general, adding hot stock will expedite this transition.

7. Once the rice is cooked, uncover it and let some of the steam escape.

8. Finish with lots of fresh parsley and a wedge of lemon. You can also choose to include okra as a healthy addition to this dish.

Creamy Red Beans

LEVEL 2   SERVINGS: 4

This dish fed me frequently during the first five years in this country. In the early days, I would use simply garam masala that I had brought with me from India, but soon after, I began becoming more confident with spices (and so can you!). This preparation of red kidney beans is a staple of North Indian cuisine. Some versions use whole black cardamom for a distinctively smokey flavor. I recommend that as well.

 HEART HEALTH NOTE: *Cuminum cyminum*, or cumin seed, have shown to possess hypolipidemic effects by reducing plasma cholesterol, LDL, and triglycerides levels. Do not confuse this with black cumin (Nigella sativa), whose cardiovascular benefits are not nearly so well-established.

½ teaspoon cumin seeds

1 large onion, minced

½-inch piece of fresh ginger, minced

4 medium garlic cloves, minced

2 fresh green chilies, minced

1 teaspoon coriander powder

½ teaspoon Kashmiri red chili powder (optional)

½ teaspoon turmeric powder

1 teaspoon Garam Masala (see page 236)

1 teaspoon dry fenugreek leaves

3 medium tomatoes, finely chopped

½ cup red wine vinegar

2 medium cans kidney beans, no-sodium, drained and rinsed well

1 cup oat milk

2 sprigs fresh cilantro, chopped

Water, as needed

Black pepper, as desired

1. In a heavy-bottomed pan, add the cumin seeds, and cook for 30 seconds.

2. Next, add the onions and brown on medium heat for 3 minutes.

3. Next, add the ginger, garlic, and green chiles. Cook for 5 minutes.

4. Now add the remaining spices and cook for 2 minutes before adding the tomatoes and red wine vinegar. Cover, and stew on low for 5 minutes or until the tomatoes break down and start creating a sauce.

5. Now add the beans and enough of the water used to cook the beans to barely cover the mixture. Cook on medium for 20 minutes until the beans start breaking down.

6. Using a ladle or spatula, smash to break down some of the beans. This gives a great depth of flavor and naturally thickens the beans.

7. Finish with oat milk cream by mixing it uniformly into the mixture. Garnish with chopped cilantro.

Quinoa & Garbanzo Pilaf

LEVEL 2   **SERVINGS: 4**

This recipe provides an amazing balance and contrast at the same time. So many powerful ingredients, so much freshness, and so versatile.

 HEART HEALTH NOTE: Walnuts decrease diastolic blood pressure and improve endothelial function. They can lower LDL cholesterol, decrease oxidative stress and reduce inflammatory markers. Walnuts are also rich in polyunsaturated fatty acids, classifying them as a calorically dense food (7 nuts = 18g total fat). In other words, consume in moderation!

- 1 cup white quinoa, washed well and rubbed under water to soften the hull, drained well
- 1 cup diced carrots
- 1 cup diced celery
- 2 cups diced onions
- 2 cups dry white wine
- 2 bay leaves
- 1 tablespoon minced garlic
- 1 teaspoon ground Hungarian paprika
- 1½ cups corn (from about 2 ears of corn)
- 2 cups cooked, ready-to-eat garbanzo beans
- 2 cups fresh tomatoes, chopped
- 2 cups unsalted vegetable stock
- ½ cup white balsamic vinegar
- 4 cups fresh spinach with tender stems
- ¼ cup dry and toasted walnuts, chopped coarsely
- ¼ cup fresh parsley, chopped finely
- Juice and zest of 1 lemon
- Freshly ground black pepper, to taste

1. In a heavy-bottomed saucepan, toast the quinoa over medium heat for about five minutes.

2. Add the carrots, celery, and onions and continue toasting for another five minutes.

3. Add the white wine and cook for two minutes. Next, add the bay leaves, garlic, and paprika. Cook for another two minutes before adding the corn and garbanzo beans.

4. After about ten minutes, stir in the tomatoes, stock, and balsamic vinegar. Taste the liquid and adjust the acidity by adding some fresh lemon juice. Cover and cook on medium heat for about ten minutes. When you see that the quinoa has split open and appears sprouted, shut off the flame and keep the dish covered for about ten minutes so that any excess liquid is absorbed.

5. Fold in the fresh spinach and parsley until the spinach just wilts.

6. Mix in any remaining lemon juice and the lemon zest.

7. Fluff with a fork before serving as a hearty lunch with a sprinkle of chopped walnuts or as the bed for some grilled or smoked vegetables for dinner.

Umami Ramen

LEVEL 2   **SERVINGS: 4**

The title of this version of ramen may be redundant. After all, ramen without umami is just a noodle and broth dish. Too often, vegetarians are left out of this experience, so I wanted to provide a canvas to develop umami via plant-based ingredients. The recipe is relatively straightforward but be sure to develop good flavor in the broth via simmering and the use of good quality ingredients.

 HEART HEALTH NOTE: Garlic, onions, shallots, leeks, and chives are among the allium class of vegetables and all have anti-platelet activity properties. They also have antioxidant activities that provide cardioprotective benefits.

1 medium skin-on white onion, quartered

2 whole heads garlic, cut in half

1-inch piece of fresh ginger, cut into slices

1 cup leeks, sliced

2 whole shallots, peeled

1 cup Napa or Savoy cabbage, chopped

1 carrot, sliced

1 cup cremini mushrooms, sliced

2 cups dry sake

½ cup nutritional yeast

1 cup rehydrated shiitake mushrooms

1 sheet kombu

1 whole star anise

1 Spiced Bouquet Garni (see page 197)

4 portions whole grain or whole wheat ramen-style noodles (no-sodium)

2 cups firm tofu, cubed

¼ cup scallions, sliced thinly

1 cup white or brown clamshell or alba mushrooms

1 cup Japanese eggplant, sliced and roasted

2 bay leaves

3 quarts water, more or less

1. For the broth, in a heavy bottomed pot on medium-high heat, brown the onion, ginger, shallots, garlic heads, leeks, cabbage, carrot, and cremini mushrooms. There is a fine line between golden brown and burnt. The ingredients have a lot of natural sugars so be careful not to burn the ingredients, especially the garlic. Reduce the heat after you see a fond developing on the bottom of the pot. Deglaze with sake and cook for a couple of minutes.

2. Next, add the nutritional yeast, rehydrated shiitake, kombu, bay leaves, and star anise. Mix well and cook for a minute before adding enough water to account for a 25% reduction and still yield about 2 quarts of strained broth. Mix all the ingredients well and add the bouquet garni. Simmer uncovered on medium low for at least two hours. Adjust the seasonings along the way to achieve the depth and balance of flavor you desire.

3. Strain the broth through a fine mesh or through several layers of cheese-cloth. If the broth is weak in flavor, transfer it to a pot and begin reducing it. This will intensify the depth of flavor.

4. To compose the ramen bowl, arrange the noodles, tofu, scallions, alba mushrooms, and roasted eggplant, in a bowl before ladling in piping hot broth. Be sure to have the noodles in the center of the bowl.

Roasted Acorn Squash with Cranberry Sauce

LEVEL 2   **SERVINGS: 4**

Stuffed hard squashes are an elevated alternative to stuffing a tomato or pepper. This dish is perfect for holidays and celebrations because the ingredients and flavors play well to provide what we are accustomed to during those moments.

 HEART HEALTH NOTE: The polyphenols found in cranberries decrease oxidative stress. Cranberries are also effective against all inflammatory processes, like vessel wall damage. Wild cranberry fruit possesses greater antioxidant properties.

- **2 medium sized acorn squash, ends trimmed, cut in half lengthwise, and seeds scooped out**
- **1 shallot or small red onion, sliced thinly**
- **2 sticks celery, chopped finely**
- **1 red bell pepper, cored, chopped finely**
- **1 tablespoon fresh thyme**

- **1 cup white quinoa, washed well, soaked for 1 hour in warm water**
- **1 cup fresh or frozen cranberries**
- **2 cups oranges, seeds removed**
- **1 cup fresh tomato, chopped**
- **2 tablespoons date syrup**
- **½ cup walnuts, chopped coarsely**
- **2 cups water**
- **Black pepper, as desired**

1. Place the acorn squash halves on a baking sheet and roast at 350°F for 45 minutes.

2. While the squash is roasting, roast the onion, celery, pepper, and thyme in a saucepan. Add the quinoa and water. Bring to a simmer, cover, and cook for 25 minutes. Leave covered.

3. As the quinoa and squash are cooking, simmer the cranberries, oranges, tomatoes, and date syrup for 15 minutes. Check the acidity and add more date syrup if desired. Blend the sauce.

4. Pack a layer of cooked quinoa inside the roasted squash. Scoop out some squash for a deeper pocket. Add the scooped squash into the quinoa mixture.

5. Drizzle the cranberry sauce on the quinoa-stuffed squash and top with chopped walnuts for a satisfying and delicious meal.

Moroccan Squash & Garbanzo Stew

LEVEL 2 SERVINGS: 4

This recipe is straightforward, but because it calls for Ras El Hanout and a spiced bouquet garni (albeit, optionally), the spice component is among the highest in the book. A reminder that *spiced* does not necessarily equal *spicy*.

 HEART HEALTH NOTE: Turmeric decreases macrophage infiltration in atherosclerosis plaque, decreases atherosclerotic lesion size, and decreases TNF-α levels — all of which help to prevent a myocardial infarction.

1 medium onion, chopped

4 cloves garlic, minced

1-inch piece fresh ginger, minced

1 cup butternut squash, cubed

1 acorn squash, washed, cored and chopped into medium-sized pieces with the skin

1 teaspoon ground turmeric

1 tablespoon Ras El Hanout (optional, see page 238)

1 Spiced Bouquet Garni (optional, see page 197)

3 medium fresh tomatoes, chopped

½ cup apple cider vinegar

2 lemons, juiced and zested

2 small cans garbanzo beans, drained and rinsed

Fresh mint, chopped

Water, as needed

Whole grain bread, as desired

Black pepper, as desired

1. In a pot, heat the onions, garlic, and ginger to a light brown.

2. Add the butternut and acorn and roast for 5 minutes.

3. Add the turmeric, Ras El Hanout, and bouquet garni. Toast for about 30 seconds.

4. Add the tomatoes, vinegar, lemon juice and lemon zest. Stew for a few minutes.

5. Now add the garbanzo beans and enough water to barely cover the ingredients. Taste the broth and adjust the acidity and spice to your preference.

6. Simmer covered for 30 minutes.

7. Garnish with fresh mint and serve with whole grain bread.

Eggplant with Herbed Brown Rice

LEVEL 2   SERVINGS: 4

A uniquely Iranian dish with Persian roots, *fesenjoon* (also *fesenjan*) simply demonstrates the expert handling of fruit, fragrance, and decadence all in one dish. It's no wonder that so many North Indian and Pakistani dishes have ancestral roots in the food of Persia. The flavors are uniquely exotic and will inspire you to learn more about Persian food. The herbed brown rice is a healthier and more nutritious take on a traditional *sabzi polo*, which uses refined long grain white rice.

 HEART HEALTH NOTE: Dairy-free oat milk contains zero cholesterol. Additionally, oat milk has B-vitamins and folate which provide cardioprotective benefits by helping to break down homocysteine circulating in the blood. It also contains β-glucans, like mushrooms, which is a source of dietary fiber.

- 4 cups water or no-sodium vegetable stock, more or less
- ¼ teaspoon turmeric
- 1 cup finely chopped dill leaves and tender stems
- 1 cup finely chopped cilantro and tender stems
- 2 sprigs fresh mint leaves, chopped
- 1 tablespoon nutritional yeast
- 1 cup brown rice
- 1 small can garbanzo, no-sodium, drained and rinsed
- 12 baby eggplant (or medium Italian eggplant chopped into large pieces), cut a cross-hatch at the base but leave intact

- ½ cup dry white wine
- 1 cup walnuts, toasted and ground
- 1 large red onion, sliced thinly
- 2 cloves garlic, minced
- ½ inch piece fresh ginger, minced
- ¾ cup pomegranate concentrate
- 1 cup finely diced leeks or shallots
- 1 cup oat milk
- Pinch of saffron, bloomed in some warm water
- Sugar, as needed
- Pomegranate seeds for garnish
- Black pepper, as desired

1. For the sabzi polo, bring 3 cups of water, turmeric, dill, cilantro, mint, nutritional yeast to a simmer. Add the brown rice and garbanzo.

2. Cover and cook on medium-low for 30–40 minutes (follow the directions on the rice package).

3. Preheat the oven to 350°F. Toss the eggplant in pepper and white wine and roast on a sheet tray until soft and golden brown (about 30 minutes)

4. In a bowl, mix the ground walnuts in some water to make a walnut paste. Meanwhile, in a pan, heat roast the onions to a golden-brown stage.

5. Add the garlic and ginger and cook for a couple of minutes.

6. Add the walnut paste, leeks or shallots, saffron water, and pomegranate concentrate to the pan. Stir in the oat milk and add some stock or water to thin out a bit. Adjust the balance of flavor.

7. Simmer on low to intensify the sauce. By now, the eggplants should be ready. Place them carefully in the sauce, spoon some sauce on each, and cover the pan. Stew the eggplant in the sauce for another 10 minutes.

Shepherd's Pie
with Roasted Brussels Sprouts

LEVEL 3   SERVINGS: 4

The only disclaimer here would be that I don't think shepherds are raising soybeans. However, I could very well be mistaken. There is so much natural depth of flavor in this humble, yet supremely comforting dish that I decided only to swap out the animal protein for a plant-based option. Pro tip: Caramelize and deglaze.

 HEART HEALTH NOTE: Brassica vegetables, including Brussels sprouts, kale, cabbage, broccoli, and cauliflower, have shown to possess important effects on the vascular system through ACE and Renin inhibitions, along with their cardioprotective nature. The Renin-angiotensin system is a major regulator of blood pressure, while ACE inhibitors are well-known for their cardioprotective mechanisms at the molecular and cellular level.

3 medium Yukon gold potatoes

2 cups oat milk

2 bay leaves

2 tablespoons ground chia seed

2 cups extra-firm tofu, chopped finely

2 cups onion, small diced

1 cup carrot, small diced

1 cup celery, small diced

4 cloves garlic, minced

1 tablespoon tomato paste

2 cups dry red wine

1 tablespoon fresh rosemary, chopped

1 tablespoon fresh thyme, chopped

1 cup fresh green peas (frozen if fresh is not available)

1 tablespoon fresh parsley, chopped

1 cup vegetable stock (no-sodium)

12 ounces fresh Brussels sprouts, ends trimmed, and halved

¼ cup apple cider vinegar

1 tablespoon Dijon mustard

½ cup chopped Macadamia nuts or walnuts, chopped coarsely

Pinch of ground nutmeg, freshly grated, if possible

Water, as needed

Black pepper, as desired

1. Boil the potatoes in water, starting in cold water. Drain well and spread on a sheet tray and dry out in a low temperature oven for 15 minutes or so. While the potatoes are drying out, heat the oat milk and one bay leaf. Season with a pinch of freshly grated nutmeg, and pepper.

2. After 15 minutes, discard the bay leaf. Transfer the cooked and dried potatoes to a bowl and in stages, add the warm oat milk to the potatoes and mash with a potato masher. Make sure the lumps are non-existent. Whisk in the ground chia seeds into the mashed potatoes.

3. In a cast-iron or heavy-bottomed skillet, brown the chopped tofu. In the same skillet, cook the mirepoix (onions, carrots, celery) until soft. Next, add the garlic and cook for a few seconds before adding the tomato paste. Cook this mixture for a couple of minutes before deglazing with the wine. Add the rosemary, thyme, and peas. If the mixture is too dry, add some stock, but it shouldn't be as wet as a broth.

4. Transfer this mixture into a baking dish (either family-style or individual portions). Spread the warm mashed potatoes on the top and bake at 375°F for 20 minutes or until the top is golden brown. Let the pie cool down significantly before finishing with the chopped parsley.

5. For the Brussels sprouts, simply roast them in a skillet until golden brown, add the vinegar, mustard, and some water. Cook uncovered until the Brussels sprouts are cooked to your liking. Finish with some black pepper.

6. Serve a portion of the pie with a serving of braised Brussels sprouts sprinkled with some nuts.

Stuffed Cabbage with Sicilian Tomato Sauce

LEVEL 3   SERVINGS: 4

This is a dish which celebrates the humble cabbage but is rarely a vegetarian dish. That's because the filling tends to have some type of meat. Well, that's an easy fix.

 HEART HEALTH NOTE: Peanuts have antioxidant properties that provide protection against cardiovascular diseases such as arteriosclerosis. Resveratrol, found in nuts, acts as a possible antiatherogenic agent and improves wound healing of the endothelium.

1 cup onion, chopped finely

½ cup carrot, chopped

½ cup celery, chopped

3 cloves garlic, minced

1 cup dry white wine

2 cups vegetable stock, no-sodium

1 cup lentils, washed well

½ cup toasted unsalted peanuts

½ teaspoon dried sage

¼ cup white balsamic

6–8 large leaves of Savoy cabbage

1 teaspoon tomato paste

½ teaspoon red chili flakes, more or less

2 cans San Marzano crushed tomatoes, no salt

1 red bell pepper, cored and chopped finely

½ teaspoon cayenne pepper (optional)

Pinch of sugar

Pinch of freshly grated nutmeg

Water for blanching the cabbage leaves

Black pepper

1. In a saucepan, roast the onion, carrots, celery, and half the garlic. Add the washed lentils and stir well. Add the white wine and cook for a minute before adding the stock. Cover and cook the lentils. It should take about 20 minutes. Allow the lentils to absorb more of the water. Drain off any excess liquid and transfer the cooked lentils to a bowl. Mix in the peanuts, nutmeg, sage, and a tablespoon of vinegar. This is the filling.

2. Blanch the cabbage leaves in water until they are pliable. Remove and allow to dry on a sheet tray. Dry the cabbage leaves and cut out any thick veins. Chop up the veins finely and add them to the lentil mixture.

3. For the sauce, cook the remaining garlic, red pepper, tomato paste, chili flakes, remaining vinegar, and the pinch of sugar for 30 minutes. Blend the sauce.

4. Place ¼ cup of filling in the middle of each blanched leaf. Roll it up, tucking in any exposed sides just like a burrito. Make all the stuffed cabbage leaves first. In a baking dish, spread a layer of tomato sauce and place the cabbage rolls evenly spaced. Pour the remaining sauce over the rolls and bake in a 375°F oven for about 20 minutes. Let them cool before serving each roll with adequate tomato sauce.

Roasted Fennel &
Butternut Squash Lasagna

LEVEL 3   SERVINGS: 4

Roasted fennel, garlic, thyme, and butternut squash have a great affinity for each other. This dish can be a good option for when you are craving a comfort-laden lasagna without the guilt of dairy or meat. Food is love and when ingredients love each other, their combination is that much more lovable.

HEART HEALTH NOTE: Consuming garlic can improve hypertension, hyper-cholesterolemia and C-reactive protein (CRP) — a marker of atherosclerosis. Garlic can also lower blood pressure and is cardioprotective. Studies have shown that raw garlic juice can improve the gut biome and reduce TMAO in just one week.

1 medium butternut squash, peeled, de-seeded, chopped into medium-sized pieces

2 bulbs fennel with stems, diced

4 sprigs fresh thyme

10 cloves garlic

4 cups canned San Marzano tomatoes with juices (no salt version)

1 bay leaf

¼ cup red wine vinegar

1 cup ground crushed almonds

2 cups oat milk

1 sprig rosemary

1 tablespoon Dijon mustard

¼ cup nutritional yeast

2 cups dry white wine

Lasagna (eggless) pasta sheets, as needed, fresh or dried

Water to cook pasta, if using dried sheets

Juice and zest of 1 lemon

Black pepper, as desired

1. Preheat the oven to 375°F and spread the butternut and fennel on a baking sheet. Toss in two sprigs of thyme and three cloves of garlic each. Season with pepper and roast for 30 minutes. Remove and let cook.

2. Make a quick marinara by cooking 4 cloves of garlic, tomatoes, bay leaf, and red wine vinegar for 20 minutes. Discard the bay leaf and blend the sauce.

3. While the vegetables are roasting, cook the pasta sheets, according to the directions if using a dried lasagna product. If you are using fresh or no-bake pasta sheets, of course, skip this step.

4. Make a white sauce by simmering the white wine, almonds, oat milk, rosemary, mustard, and nutritional yeast. Discard the rosemary. Add the lemon juice, lemon zest, and some black pepper before blending the sauce.

5. Chop up the roasted garlic and pick the roasted thyme leaves for the lasagna. Coarsely chop up the roasted fennel and mix in the chopped roasted garlic and thyme. Prepare an appropriately-sized baking pan for the lasagna.

6. Alternate layers of marinara, pasta, roasted butternut, roasted garlic and fennel, pasta, white sauce, roasted fennel, etc. Be sure to end with marinara dotted with some white sauce. Bake at 375°F, first covered for 30 minutes, then uncovered for 30 minutes. Allow the pasta to rest for at least 30 minutes before portioning and serving.

Assorted Mushroom Moussaka

LEVEL 3   SERVINGS: 4

Non-vegetarian moussaka is well known, but this earthy and full-bodied variation is a delicious alternative. In general, dishes like moussaka are conducive to many variations. Whoever thought of topping off a dish with a fluffy, soufflé-like crust was a genius. And the eggplant and white beans provide a deliciously savory alternative to meat.

 HEART HEALTH NOTE: Consumption of flax seed is associated with a lower prevalence of hypertension and lower systolic blood pressure. Flax seed is high in omega-3 fatty acids and can replace fish oils as a supplement. These seeds also reduce levels of LDL and TC. Alpha-linolenic acid (ALA), found in flax seeds, have cholesterol-lowering actions similar to most statin medications.

2–4 medium-sized eggplant, partially skinned

3 cups assorted mushrooms, chopped

2 cups white wine

2 medium onions, minced

4 cloves garlic, minced

1 tablespoon tomato paste

1 can chopped tomatoes, no-sodium

2 tablespoons flat-leaf parsley

6 cups oat milk

2 bay leaves

½ teaspoon grated or ground nutmeg

2 ounces flax meal

2 Yukon gold potatoes, cooked and riced or grated

½ cup unsalted breadcrumbs

1 can white beans, no-sodium

2 tablespoons fresh oregano

2 tablespoons tapioca starch slurry (see page 23)

Water, as needed

Black pepper, as desired

1. Slice eggplants lengthwise and roast them on a baking sheet with mushrooms until soft and golden brown (about 25 minutes at 350°F).

2. In a saucepan, cook the white wine, 1 cup onions, garlic, tomato paste, chopped tomato, and parsley. Simmer until thick.

3. Add the slurry to the oat milk, remaining onions, bay leaves, and nutmeg. Simmer until you achieve a smooth creamy sauce without the starchiness. Discard the bay leaves and whisk in the flax meal before pouring over the cooked potatoes. Mash well and add more herbs if desired.

4. In a baking dish, sprinkle some seasoned breadcrumbs. Place a layer of the eggplants and mushroom mixture and sprinkle some oregano.

5. Next, spread a few white beans and tomato sauce.

6. Repeat layers until all is used ensuring that the last layer is eggplant. Spread the creamy potato over the top and bake uncovered at 350–375°F until very hot throughout and the sauce is set and browned (approx. 55–60 minutes).

7. Let it cool for at least 15 minutes before portioning and serving.

Desserts

AFTER A SATISFYING DINNER, the perfect ending is an easy, light, and perfectly sweet dessert. When that dessert is both decadent and heart-healthy, it enhances the promise of a better, healthier tomorrow. This section offers six versatile recipes that are easy to prepare, providing a multitude of enjoyable variations.

Dark Chocolate & Walnut Brownies

LEVEL 1   **SERVINGS: 16**

I recommend using a high-quality dark chocolate for this recipe. Beyond that, it is a straightforward recipe.

 HEART HEALTH NOTE: Studies on the consumption of chocolate products rich in cocoa flavanols and flavan-3-ols found reduced incidence of CVD events like stroke and ischemic heart disease. Unfortunately, these effects are probably counteracted by the high fat content, especially saturated fat. While the epicatechin in cocoa can increase vasodilation and lower blood pressure in much smaller amounts, its use may not be practical in everyday life.

½ cup whole wheat flour

1½ cups all-purpose flour

1 cup granulated sugar

¾ cup unsweetened cocoa powder

¼ teaspoon cream of tartar

¼ cup dark chocolate chips

1 teaspoon ground cinnamon

1 teaspoon baking powder

2 cups oat milk

1 tablespoon vanilla extract

1 cup walnuts, chopped

1. Preheat the oven to 350°F.

2. Spray a 13 x 9-inch baking sheet with a small amount of fat-free cooking spray.

3. In a bowl, mix the flour, sugar, cream of tartar, cocoa powder, cinnamon, and baking powder.

4. Mix the vanilla extract and oat milk. Pour over the dried ingredients and mix well.

5. Fold in the walnuts and dark chocolate.

6. Pour batter into the baking dish and bake for about 30 minutes.

7. Cool for at least 30 minutes, before portioning the brownies.

Chia & Banana Pudding

LEVEL 1   **SERVINGS: 4**

Once you get used to the texture and flavor of a chia-based pudding, you will become comfortable making a wide variety of flavored puddings. Also, they can be made ahead of time during prep day and refrigerated.

 HEART HEALTH NOTE: Chia is an excellent source of α-linolenic acid and has a high percentage of fatty acids. These omega-3 fatty acids improve cholesterol levels, parasympathetic tone, and are cardioprotective. They can decrease diastolic blood pressure and triglyceride levels. (Note that chia and flax seeds together have even stronger cardiovascular benefits.)

2 ripe bananas, cut into small pieces

¼ cup date syrup

¼ teaspoon cream of tartar

½ teaspoon ground cinnamon

½ teaspoon vanilla extract

1½ cups unsweetened almond milk or coconut milk

½ cup chia seeds

1 cup chilled blueberries

1. In a bowl, mix the banana, cream of tartar, date syrup, ground cinnamon, and vanilla. Add the almond or coconut milk a bit at a time until you have a smooth mixture.

2. Whisk in the chia seeds, cover, and refrigerate for about 4 hours. Whisk the mixture once after about an hour of refrigeration.

3. Serve chilled with blueberries on top.

Strawberry & Coconut Ice-Cream

LEVEL 1   SERVINGS: 4

There is a proliferation of dairy-free ice-creams in the grocery stores these days. However, barring a few brands, the nutritional labels for the vast majority still indicate high levels of saturated fat. It should be noted that this recipe calls for coconut cream, which does contain some saturated fat. So, if you want to avoid even that amount, I recommend substituting oat milk or cashew milk for coconut milk.

 HEART HEALTH NOTE: Strawberries are abundant in ellagic acid and the flavonoids anthocyanin, catechin, and quercetin. They inhibit LDL oxidation, reduce thrombosis formation, and improve endothelial function. Many studies have concluded that daily strawberry or blueberry consumption may have a positive effect on health.

10 ounces frozen strawberries

1 ripe banana, sliced and chilled

1 teaspoon vanilla extract

¼ teaspoon cream of tartar

1 cup coconut cream, canned

1 tablespoon date syrup

1. Pulse the strawberries, banana, and vanilla in a food processor.

2. Add the cream of tartar, coconut cream, and date syrup. Process to a smooth texture.

3. Store in a covered container in the freezer for at least 2 hours before serving.

Glazed Bananas with Walnut Crumb

LEVEL 1   **SERVINGS: 4**

This recipe is inspired by the classic Bananas Foster and, if desired, one may serve this dessert with a plant-based, low-fat ice cream or sorbet.

 HEART HEALTH NOTE: Bananas are high in soluble fiber and have positive effects on systolic BP and CRP plasma concentration. Walnuts are a good source of alpha-linolenic acid (ALA), an omega-3 fatty acid that has been associated with reductions in inflammation and improvements in cardiovascular risk factors such as high systolic blood pressure and C-reactive protein (CRP) levels in the plasma, further supporting heart health.

4 firm but ripe bananas, peeled and sliced lengthwise

½ cup light brown sugar, divided

1 teaspoon cinnamon powder, divided

1 teaspoon vanilla extract

¼ cup dark rum

½ cup unsalted walnuts

1 cup water

1. In a shallow large pan, combine the bananas, ¼ cup brown sugar, ½ teaspoon cinnamon, vanilla, and rum. Bring to a low simmer.

2. Using a torch, flame the mixture carefully so that the alcohol in the rum evaporates. Optionally, cooking the bananas a bit longer will allow the alcohol to evaporate, naturally.

3. As the bananas are becoming glazed, toast the walnuts in a dry pan for 5 minutes on medium heat, stirring periodically.

4. In a food processor, combine the toasted walnuts, ¼ cup brown sugar, and ½ teaspoon cinnamon. Pulse a few times to achieve a coarse crumb.

5. Sprinkle the walnut crumb on the glazed bananas.

Fresh Fruit with Walnuts, Fresh Herbs & Date Syrup

LEVEL 1   SERVINGS: 4

I saved the simplest dessert for the end to illustrate how a few good ingredients can provide a memorable ending to a deliciously-good-for-you, heart-healthy, whole food, plant-based meal.

 HEART HEALTH NOTE: Bananas are a great source of potassium. A high potassium intake may reduce high blood pressure and has been linked to a lower risk of stroke and heart disease. Bananas are also a good source of soluble and insoluble dietary fiber and assist in glucose and cholesterol adsorption, along with stimulating probiotic growth. Apples, meanwhile, have epicatechin, a flavan-3-ol that stimulates the NO pathway, activates the eNOS pathway and increases vasodilation.

4 cups assorted fruit (blueberries, apples, strawberries, banana, and orange segments)

1 lime, juice and zest

¼ cup date syrup

½ cup mixture of fresh basil and tarragon, and chopped without bruising

½ cup walnuts, chopped

1. In a bowl, mix the fruit, lime juice and zest, basil, and date syrup. Allow the mixture to marinate for 30 minutes.

2. Serve in a bowl sprinkled with walnuts.

Oatmeal & Berry Cobbler

LEVEL 2   SERVINGS: 4

Cobblers are Southern staples and a wonderful way to showcase in-season fruits like peaches, plums, apples, and cherries. This version makes use of berries, which are available year-round in grocery stores.

 HEART HEALTH NOTE: Strawberries, blueberries, and blackberries are high in antioxidants, fiber, and heart-healthy phytonutrients. Additionally, switching from cow's milk to almond milk can contribute to cardiovascular health, by reducing calories and saturated fats, to manage cholesterol levels.

4 cups assorted berries, washed and dried

Juice and zest of 1 lemon

½ cup granulated sugar, divided

¼ cup almond milk

¾ cup all-purpose flour

½ teaspoon baking powder

¼ cup plant-based, no-sodium butter

1 cup quick-cooking oats

¼ cup chopped walnuts

¼ cup light brown sugar

1 teaspoon cinnamon powder

Fat-free plant-based sorbet (optional)

1. In a bowl, combine the berries with the lemon juice, lemon zest, and half the sugar. Set aside for 10 minutes.

2. In a different bowl, combine flour, almond milk, remaining sugar, and baking powder to form a thick batter. Adjust the amount of liquid to ensure that the batter is thick.

3. Lightly cream the brown sugar, cinnamon, and butter. Fold in the oats and walnuts.

4. Preheat the oven to 375°F.

5. Place the berry mixture in a uniform layer inside a baking dish.

6. Pour the batter uniformly.

7. Place dollops of the oat mixture in various spots on the batter.

8. Bake for about 45 minutes or until golden brown and bubbly.

9. Allow the cobbler to cool for 10 minutes before serving. Serve with a fat-free plant-based sorbet, if preferred.

Ginger-Spiced Baked Grapefruit

LEVEL 1   **SERVINGS: 4**

A fresh grapefruit is a common breakfast option and a delicious one at that. This recipe shows how one can elevate the same idea by using a few spices and accenting flavors.

 HEART HEALTH NOTE: The flavonoids found in grapefruit decrease cholesterol, positively affect the NO pathway, improve basal endothelial function and reduce oxidative stress. Naringin, a grapefruit flavonoid, can also increase endothelium flow.

2 large grapefruit, sliced in half along the equator

1 tablespoon date syrup

1 teaspoon fresh ginger, grated or minced

¼ teaspoon ground cardamom

1 teaspoon light date powder

1. Preheat the oven to 400°F.
2. Brush the flesh of the grapefruit with date syrup.
3. Sprinkle the ginger, cardamom, and light date powder on the flesh of the sliced grapefruit.
4. Bake on a sheet tray for about 15 minutes.
5. Allow the baked grapefruit to cool a bit before enjoying as is or with a dollop of fat-free, non-dairy ice cream or yogurt.

Pantry

THIS SECTION WILL HELP you create plant-based alternatives to traditional staples and teach you the basics of infusing dishes with delicious flavor. Beans and legumes are crucial to a heart-healthy, plant-based diet, and learning to properly prepare dried beans ensures not only more flavorful meals but also avoids the preservatives and over-processing found in canned beans.

Classic Bouquet Garni

LEVEL 1

Cheese cloth
2 thyme springs
1 bunch parsley stems
2 bay leaves
6 whole peppercorns
String or twine

1. Fill a cheese cloth with two thyme sprigs, one bunch of parsley stems, 2 bay leaves, and 6 whole peppercorns.

2. Make a pouch and tie it with a string or twine long enough to be able to tie to the handle of a vessel. If making ahead on your prep day, be sure to keep it refrigerated until you need it for a dish.

What's a Bouquet Garni?

This refers to a cheesecloth pouch filled with aromatics and secured by tying a knot with a twine. Make sure there is enough lead line twine to be able to tie the pouch to the handle of a pot and submerge the aromatics into a broth or sauce. After the aromatics have infused the liquid during the simmering stage, it is easy to untie or cut the knot and discard the bouquet garni.

Spiced Bouquet Garni

LEVEL 1

Cheese cloth
2 cinnamon sticks
2 bay leaves
1 whole black cardamom
6 whole coriander seeds
5 whole fennel seeds
4 whole green or white
    cardamoms
4 whole cloves
5 whole peppercorns
2 whole cloves garlic
½-inch piece fresh ginger

1. Fill a cheese cloth with two cinnamon sticks, 2 bay leaves, 1 whole black cardamom, 6 whole coriander seeds, 5 whole fennel seeds, 4 whole green or white cardamoms, 4 whole cloves, 5 whole peppercorns, 2 whole cloves of garlic, and ½-inch piece of fresh ginger.

2. Make a pouch and tie it with a string or twine long enough to be able to tie to the handle of a vessel. If making ahead on your prep day, be sure to keep it refrigerated until you need it for a dish.

Aquafaba

LEVEL 1   **YIELD: ABOUT 2 CUPS**

HEART HEALTH NOTE: This is a neutral base, a blank slate, and almost calorie free with only 3 calories per tablespoon. The concentration of everything else is too low to list.

Liquid from one 15-ounce
    can no-sodium
    chickpeas
⅛ teaspoon cream
    of tartar

1. Gather the liquid into a large mixing bowl or mixer.

2. Add the cream of tartar.

3. Using a hand or stand mixer, whip for about 10 minutes to the desired thickness.

4. Use immediately or store in the refrigerator for a day or two. Re-whip, if necessary.

Flaxseed Gel

 HEART HEALTH NOTE: Flaxseed is a cardiovascular dietary workhorse. Among the richest sources of α-linolenic acid, it also contains Omega-3 fatty acids, is high in fiber, provides protein, lowers cholesterol, and possesses antihypertensive action.

1 tablespoon ground flaxseed

3 tablespoon warm water

1. Add the ground flaxseed to the water and whisk with a fork or whip for about 2 minutes.

2. Allow the mixture to stand for about 10 minutes until it gets gelatinous.

3. Use immediately, or store in the refrigerator for another day.

4. Rehydrate if it congeals too much.

Chia Gel

 HEART HEALTH NOTE: Chia is an excellent source of α-linolenic acid and contains a high percentage of fatty acids. In studies, chia seeds have reduced pulse rates in patients with hypertension.

¼ cup chia seeds

1¼ cups water

1. Mix the chia seeds and water in a bowl or jar.

2. Shake the mixture for about 30 seconds.

3. Let it rest for about 10 minutes until it becomes gelatinous.

4. Use immediately, or store in the refrigerator for another day.

Mild Cheese Substitute

MOZZARELLA-STYLE

LEVEL 1   YIELD: **EQUIVALENT OF 2 CUPS**

 HEART HEALTH NOTE: Nutritional yeast is a dietary supplement that is a good source of B-vitamins, including: thiamine (B1), riboflavin (B2), niacin (B3), and B6 and B12. Increased vitamin B6 levels are associated with a reduced risk of ischemic stroke. Riboflavin is a potent B-vitamin to reduce blood pressure. B-vitamins decrease in oxidative stress, including homocysteine.

1 cup raw cashew nuts soaked in hot water for 2 hours

½ cup oat milk

3 tablespoon nutritional yeast

2 ounces tapioca starch

Juice of 1 lemon

Water, as needed

1. Blend the soaked cashews with the remaining ingredients until creamy and smooth.

2. Cook the mixture on medium heat, whisking periodically as the mixture begins to bubble.

3. Continue stirring, scraping the bottom for about 5–10 minutes. Adjust the acidity as needed.

4. Transfer to a bowl and allow to cool.

5. Once cooled, the cheese substitute is ready to use or be stored in the refrigerator.

Tangy Cheese Substitute

GOAT-STYLE

LEVEL 1   YIELD: **EQUIVALENT OF 1½ CUPS**

 HEART HEALTH NOTE: Macadamia nuts are high in potassium, thiamine, ribo-flavin, retinol, and niacin. They are also a good source of magnesium, with higher serum magnesium levels being associated with lower blood pressure. Additionally, they are a source of fiber and can reduce oxidative stress, serum cholesterol and LDL.

½ cup macadamia nuts, soaked in hot water for two hours

½ cup cashew nuts, soaked in hot water for two hours

½ cup lemon juice

2 tablespoons unfiltered apple cider vinegar

Water, as needed

1. Blend the soaked macadamias and cashews with the remaining ingredients until creamy and smooth.

2. Transfer to a bowl or jar.

3. Cover and leave in a warm area for 24 hours.

4. If there is extra liquid, strain through a cheese cloth the next day.

5. The cheese substitute is ready to use or to store in the refrigerator.

Sharp Cheese Substitute

CHEDDAR-STYLE

LEVEL 1   **YIELD: EQUIVALENT OF 1½ CUPS**

HEART HEALTH NOTE: Curcumin is a polyphenolic compound found in turmeric spice, a root in the ginger family. Turmeric can modulate several pathways involved in the pathogenesis of cardiovascular disease. It can reduce lipids, decrease plaque formation, and is cardioprotective — to name just a few of its benefits.

1 cup cashew nuts, soaked in hot water for two hours

¼ cup nutritional yeast

2 tablespoons unfiltered apple cider vinegar

1 teaspoon paprika

½ teaspoon ground turmeric

1 teaspoon onion powder

½ teaspoon mustard powder

Water, as needed

1. Blend the soaked nuts and remaining ingredients until you obtain a smooth mixture.

2. Cover and refrigerate for 6–8 hours until the mixture firms up.

3. If there is extra liquid, strain through a cheese cloth the next day.

4. The cheese substitute is ready to use or be stored in the refrigerator.

Cooking Dried Beans

LEVEL 1   **YIELD: VARIES**

No two beans are alike. However, there are some simple guidelines to ensure that if you decide to cook them yourself, the process will seem less tedious and certainly more rewarding.

1. Soak the beans overnight in enough water. The water level should be above the level of beans by at least 6-inches.

2. Transfer the beans to a heavy pot.

3. Add a bouquet garni (see page 196) of your choice to the pot.

4. Add more water. It is not entirely necessary to drain the soaking water.

5. Bring the beans to a simmer and begin skimming off any foam that begins to rise to the surface.

6. Cook until the beans are tender (it can take anywhere from 1–3 hours).

7. Discard the bouquet garni and drain the cooked beans into a colander.

8. The beans are ready to use right away or can be stored in the refrigerator for a few days. You may also use some of the cooking liquid to make an aquafaba (see page 197).

Sauces & Marinades

SAUCES FORM THE FOUNDATION of flavorful cooking. Professionals depend on sauces to make their culinary creations exciting and satisfying. In classic French cooking, the sauces derived from mother sauces tend to be rich, heavy, and often depend on animal-based ingredients. In this section, you will find a wide assortment of deeply flavored sauces. Some of these are used in recipes elsewhere in this book to inspire you to change things up for yourself and become proficient and self-sufficient in this very important aspect of good cooking. Once you become comfortable with the notion of either making these sauces for a recipe or as a go-to refrigerator item to make quick weekday meals, you will notice that your overall cooking proficiency will continue to strengthen.

Pineapple Habanero
LATIN/CARIBBEAN

LEVEL 1   **YIELD: APPROXIMATELY 1 QUART**

One may substitute any juicy, fresh fruit for the pineapple. I have often used black-berry as a substitute for pineapple. The finesse lies in reducing the sauce enough while balancing it with enough sugar. The sauce, which is punchy and fruity with versatile but focused flavors, is best with any tropically influenced dish.

 HEART HEALTH NOTE: Pineapple fruit has proteolytic enzyme (referred to as fruit bromelain), an anti-inflammatory with anticoagulation factors that cause thrombus destruction, decrease red blood cell clumping and decrease blood viscosity.

1 whole fresh pineapple cut in pieces

2 bay leaves (fresh, if available)

2 sprigs fresh rosemary

3 sprigs fresh thyme

3 whole cloves garlic

2 habanero peppers, cut in half

4 quarts water

1 cup sugar

1. Simmer all the ingredients in a heavy-bottomed stainless pot for 1 hour.

2. Blend with a hand blender.

3. Strain through a fine strainer into a saucepan.

4. Simmer slowly until the liquid reduces by half.

5. To finish the sauce, test the seasoning to find a balance. Add more sugar if necessary.

6. Store in the refrigerator for up to a week.

Mojo

LATIN/CARIBBEAN

LEVEL 1   YIELD: **APPROXIMATELY 2½ CUPS**

Typically, *mojo* is most commonly used as a marinade rather than a sauce. It is undoubtedly a deliciously vibrant marinade for ingredients prior to grilling. However, when cooked on a low heat and balanced with seasonings or dairy, it may be used as a delicious sauce.

 HEART HEALTH NOTE: The main flavonoids present in citrus fruits are hesperidin and naringin. They have a strong influence on the gut biome as they are resistant to enzymatic breakdown in the stomach and small intestine, meaning they reach the colon intact. They boost *Lactobacillus* and reduce carnitine, ultimately reducing plasma TMAO.

10 cloves garlic, minced
1 cup fresh sour orange juice
    (substitute a combination of
    ½ cup of fresh orange juice and
    ½ cup of fresh lime juice)
½ teaspoon Dijon mustard
½ teaspoon dried oregano

½ teaspoon fresh oregano
½ cup cilantro stems
¾ teaspoon cumin powder
1 teaspoon Adobo Seasoning
    (see page 245)

1. Blend all ingredients in a blender.
2. Store in the refrigerator for up to a week.

Creole Marinade

LOUISIANA

LEVEL 2   **YIELD: APPROXIMATELY 2 QUARTS**

Over the years, any dish labeled *creole* seemed to instantly draw in curious diners at the restaurant. And why not?! Alongside deep-flavored sauces from India, China, Thailand, and many countries in North Africa, to name only a few, the food from Louisiana promises big and bold flavors. It is completely reasonable and possible to make creole and Cajun inspired dishes while sticking to only vegetarian ingredients. This sauce is a good starting place for that journey.

 HEART HEALTH NOTE: Lycopene is found in tomatoes, and is what gives them their distinctive color. It is cardioprotective and interferes with the inflammation reaction within blood vessels. It can inhibit platelet aggregation, reducing the total cholesterol content through the expression of HMG-CoA reductase.

2 cups medium onion, diced

1 cup celery, diced

1 cup green and red bell peppers, diced

3 sprigs fresh thyme, leaves picked

1 sprig fresh rosemary, leaves picked, chopped

3 cloves fresh garlic, minced

2 tablespoons Creole Seasoning (see page 247)

2 bay leaves, fresh if available

1 teaspoon freshly ground black pepper

2 cup ripe tomatoes, diced

1 quart water

2 tablespoons red wine vinegar

½ cup flat-leaf parsley, chopped finely

1. Over medium heat in a saucepan, cook the onions, celery, and bell peppers until they are soft and slightly caramelized.

2. Next, add the fresh thyme, rosemary, and minced garlic. Stir briefly for about a minute being careful that the garlic doesn't burn.

3. Next, add the creole blend of spices, black pepper, and bay leaves. Stir for a few seconds.

4. Add the tomatoes, vinegar, and water. Let the sauce simmer for about 30 minutes, stirring periodically.

5. Discard the bay leaf.

6. Finish with chopped, fresh flat-leaf parsley.

7. Store in the refrigerator for up to a week.

Green Curry Concentrate
THAILAND

LEVEL 2   YIELD: **APPROXIMATELY 3 CUPS**

Overall, this is a starter "Thai" curry base. Familiar and satisfying. You may increase the amount of lemongrass and manage the number of chilies based on your preference and tolerance for pungent food.

 HEART HEALTH NOTE: Reactive oxygen species (ROS) have a physiological role in controlling cardiovascular homeostasis. Citral is a flavoring compound present in lemongrass and is an antioxidant, radical scavenger, and anti-inflammatory that decreases the activity of ROS.

2 tablespoons coriander seeds

2 teaspoons cumin seeds

½ teaspoon turmeric powder

4 Thai green chilies, chopped

2 green bell peppers, seeded and chopped

4 shallots, diced

4 garlic cloves, chopped

1-inch piece of fresh ginger, chopped

5 kaffir lime leaves, chopped (use lime zest, as a substitute)

4 tablespoons chopped cilantro leaves

2 tablespoons chopped cilantro roots

2 tablespoons chopped lemongrass

½-inch piece of fresh galangal, finely chopped

¼ cup rice wine vinegar

1 cup tamarind water (tamarind fruit soaked in warm water for 20 minutes, squeezed, strained)

1. First roast the coriander and cumin in a dry frying pan over moderate heat, stirring frequently, until they just start to brown. Be careful not to burn them or they will be bitter.

2. Grind the spices before adding remaining ingredients in a blender or food processor and process until you have a smooth, free-flowing paste. Add water as needed to assist in the blending.

3. Transfer the paste to a sauté pan, heat it and simmer for 30 minutes, stirring occasionally.

4. The concentrate may be used immediately or stored in a jar in the refrigerator or even frozen.

Mushroom Demi

FRANCE

LEVEL 2   YIELD: **APPROXIMATELY 2 QUARTS**

Classically, a *demi-glace* is an intensely reduced and fortified stock—and a very specific kind at that. On contemporary restaurant menus, the used of the word *demi* implies a reduction of sorts usually by at least half. Here, I offer a fairly simple sauce in the style of a reduction. Use in pasta dishes and as a base for an earthy gravy.

 HEART HEALTH NOTE: Lycopene belongs to a broader family of lipid soluble antioxidants, called carotenoids, which have cardioprotective effects against oxidative stress. This increases the endothelium function found in tomato paste, which has been found to contain the most stable compound for lycopene levels.

1 cup dried porcini mushrooms

1 cup drled shiltake mushrooms (available in Asian markets)

3 cups cremini mushrooms, sliced

3 cloves garlic, minced

2 sprigs fresh thyme

1 sprig fresh rosemary

1 shallot, minced

2 bay leaves (preferably fresh)

1 cup oat milk

1 tablespoon whole wheat flour

2 teaspoons tomato paste

4 cups dry red wine

4 cups warm water

1. Wash the dried mushrooms well in cold water. Typically, porcini mushrooms tend to have sand and dirt. Rehydrate the dried porcini and shiitake in the warm water for about 30 minutes. Squeeze the mushrooms and carefully strain the water taking care that any sediment and sand is discarded. Keep the mushroom-infused water and chop the rehydrated mushrooms.

2. In a heavy-bottomed pot, heat the shallots and garlic for about 5 minutes on medium heat.

3. Add the flour and cook the mixture, stirring frequently for about 10 minutes until the flour turns light brown.

4. Add the fresh herbs and tomato paste. Cook for about a minute.

5. Add all the mushrooms and cook for 15 minutes.

6. Add the wine, bay leaves, and mushroom water and bring to a simmer. Season with pepper.

7. Reduce the sauce by about half the volume.

8. Add the oat milk and mix well.

9. After it cools a bit, discard the herb stems and bay leaves.

10. Blend the sauce to a smooth consistency and use immediately or store in the refrigerator for up to 5 days.

Tikka Masala

UK/INDIA

LEVEL 2   **YIELD: APPROXIMATELY 3 QUARTS**

The quintessential "Indian" curry—*not*. An invention resulting from the British Raj, chicken tikka masala is a wonderfully balanced dish. It is a starter "Indian" curry base. Familiar and satisfying to anyone who enjoys spiced tomato sauces.

 HEART HEALTH NOTE: Lycopene is used for its lipid-soluble nature; therefore, consuming it along with some fat enhances it bioavailability. Tomatoes increase levels of Vitamins A, C, K+ and improve arterial vasodilation via endothelial function.

- 1 cinnamon stick
- 5 whole cloves
- 4 whole cardamom pods
- 1 teaspoon cumin seed
- 1 teaspoon coriander seed
- 2 bay leaves, crushed
- 6 fresh curry leaves (if available)
- 1 large green bell pepper, cored, diced
- 2 large red onions, peeled, diced
- 1 tablespoon minced fresh ginger
- 4 cloves garlic, minced
- 32 ounces high-quality crushed tomatoes (avoid anything with citric acid)
- 8 ounces water or vegetable stock
- 1 teaspoon dried fenugreek leaves, crushed
- 1 tablespoon ground cumin
- 1 tablespoon ground turmeric
- 1 teaspoon ground coriander
- 1 teaspoon cayenne pepper powder (more if preferred)
- Granulated sugar, to taste

1. In a heavy-bottomed pot, heat the cinnamon sticks, cloves, cardamom, cumin seeds, and coriander seeds and stir for a minute.

2. Add the curry leaves, diced bell pepper, and onions. Cook on low to medium-low heat until the onions are lightly brown. This will take about 20 minutes.

3. Now add the fresh ginger and garlic as well as all the remaining spices. Stir well.

4. Add the ground cumin, ground turmeric, ground coriander, and cayenne pepper powder.

5. Add sugar for balance.

6. Next, add the crushed tomatoes and water/stock. Test the seasoning for balance.

7. Simmer on low for one hour, stirring periodically.

8. Add the dried fenugreek leaves. Allow the sauce to cool a bit.

9. If your blender is not powerful, remove the cinnamon sticks and discard. Otherwise, simply blend the entire mixture to a very smooth consistency.

10. Store in the refrigerator for up to a week.

Vindaloo

INDIA

LEVEL 2   **YIELD: APPROXIMATELY 2½ QUARTS**

A *vindaloo* is what happened when the foodies of colonial Portugal interacted with the locals in Goa and surrounding regions. During the Portuguese rule of parts of India, peppers, tomatoes, wine, and even vinegar were introduced to the region. Combining those with indigenous ingredients like seafood, meats, coconut, kokum, and of course spices, resulted in the birth of this beloved curry for those who like pungent food. Use this sauce when you want a zippy "Indian" red curry.

 HEART HEALTH NOTE: Fenugreek, one of the oldest phytomedicines, reduces the activity of LDL and increases HDL and HDL/LDL, giving it the potential benefit of improving atherosclerosis and hyperlipidemia. Trigonelline, a compound in fenugreek, can interfere with the conversion of TMA to TMAO. TMAO has been shown to induce atherosclerosis.

2 tablespoons whole cumin seeds

2 tablespoons whole coriander seeds

2 tablespoons fresh ginger, minced

10 cloves garlic, minced

2 large onions, diced

1 tablespoon turmeric powder

2 whole dried bay leaves

5–6 dried red chilies

1 teaspoon ground cayenne pepper

1 teaspoon ground cumin

1 teaspoon ground coriander

1 tablespoon dried fenugreek leaves

1 teaspoon smoked paprika

12-ounce can San Marzano tomatoes

½ cup red wine vinegar

2–3 cups water, more or less

1 tablespoon light date powder

1 teaspoon freshly ground black pepper

1. The method is very similar to that of Tikka Masala. The difference is in the timing of the blooming of ingredients.

2. Heat a heavy-bottomed pot and toast the whole spices. Stir continuously to not burn the spices.

3. After a few minutes, add the ginger and garlic and fry the combination until the garlic browns a bit.

4. Next, add the onions, mix well, and cook on a low heat for 20 minutes, stirring periodically.

5. Now add the remaining spices, mix well, and cook for a few minutes.

6. Now add the tomatoes, vinegar, date powder, and some water.

7. The sauce must be deeply spiced, spicy and tangy with a balanced background of sweetness.

8. Cook this sauce low and slow for about 45 minutes before blending smoothly.

9. Store in the refrigerator for up to a week.

Chutneys & Relishes

In India, a chutney can be made from just about any vegetable or fruit with a few spices. These creations offer the convenience of good refrigerator life coupled with flavors that sing. The recipes here are a diverse assortment of heart-healthy ingredients, textures, and applications. Every item in this section can be used as a spread, dipping sauce, in tacos or burritos, in sandwiches, in soups, and of course, as an accompaniment with your meal.

Salsa Verde

MEXICO/INDIA

LEVEL 1   YIELD: **APPROXIMATELY 1 QUART**

You know how cuisines of Europe, especially the Mediterranean, have salsa verde? You know how Mexican and South American cuisines have salsa verde? Well, this is a different concoction altogether. I think you will be impressed. It tastes good with just about anything and, moreover, is a great catch-all for wilted herbs and leaves of many vegetables. Used for tacos and sandwiches or as a bright, herbaceous accent on composed dishes, the salsa stays fresh and vibrant in the refrigerator for up to a week.

 HEART HEALTH NOTE: Cashew nuts are high in magnesium (Mg), and circulating Mg is associated with lower risk of ischemic heart disease and/or coronary heart disease. Vinegar lowers cholesterol and improves heart health.

1 cup cashew nut, toasted

2 lemons, zested and juiced

2 limes, zested and juiced

4 cloves garlic, peeled

1 tablespoon extra-virgin olive oil

¼ cup date syrup

¼ cup white or golden balsamic vinegar

1 tablespoon skin-on ginger, minced

2 tablespoons Dijon mustard

1 bunch basil leaves with tender stems, washed

1 bunch cilantro with stems, washed and roughly chopped

1 bunch flat-leaf parsley with stems, washed and roughly chopped

1 jalapeño (with seeds), chopped

Granulated sugar, as needed

1. In a food processor, grind the nuts until they are a fine crumb.

2. Add the citrus juices and zest, garlic, olive oil, date syrup, vinegar, ginger, and mustard. Process well.

3. Add remaining ingredients. Puree well.

4. Taste the chutney and adjust the flavor levels, as desired.

5. Store in the refrigerator for up to 1 month.

Hot Chili Paste (Harissa)

TUNISIA

LEVEL 1   YIELD: **APPROXIMATELY 1 CUP**

Harissa has become associated with North African cuisines. When you want to spice up North African dishes covering the cuisines of Algeria, Libya, Morocco, and Tunisia, I find that harissa, more than any standard hot condiment, is the appropriate option. Nowadays, it is even commonly available tableside in casual Middle Eastern restaurants to help spice up a falafel or gyro wrap.

 HEART HEALTH NOTE: Cumin, coriander, fennel, and dill seeds belong to the *Apiaceae* family of plants, having some of the healthiest fatty acid profiles around. They help to positively control hypocholesterolemia, fatty acids, atherogenesis and the thrombogenic activity. Each one is also an exceptionally rich source of mono-unsaturated fatty acids (MUFAs) in the form of petroselinic acid with a very small amount of SFAs.

3 tablespoons coriander seeds

3 tablespoons cumin seeds

1 tablespoon sumac powder

2 tablespoons dried crushed red pepper

4 garlic cloves

6 tablespoons Hungarian sweet paprika (may substitute hot paprika)

1 teaspoon smoked paprika

2 tablespoons red wine vinegar

Water, as needed

1. Toast the cumin and coriander seeds in a dry pan over medium heat for 3 minutes.

2. Add all ingredients to a food processor and whirl together until smooth.

3. Add the red wine vinegar and enough water to make a smooth paste.

4. Store in the refrigerator for up to 1 month.

Chimichurri

ARGENTINA

LEVEL 1   YIELD: **APPROXIMATELY ½ QUART**

Traditionally, chimichurri is paired with a grilled protein. My interpretation has complementary herbs and spice. I recommend using it alongside grilled vegetables or mushrooms.

 HEART HEALTH NOTE: Dijon mustard is made from brown mustard seeds and white wine. Mustard oil groups have been shown to induce a significant reduction in total cardiac arrhythmias, left ventricular enlargement and angina. They belong to the Brassicaceae family of vegetables and herbs and are widely used for sprouting and microgreen production.

2 cups fresh flat-leaf parsley (with some stems)

½ cup fresh basil

2 cloves fresh garlic

1 jalapeño or serrano pepper, more if desired

1 teaspoon Dijon mustard

1 teaspoon ground cumin

¼ cup red wine vinegar

Juice and zest of 1 lemon

1. Blend all the ingredients in a food processor to a smooth consistency.

2. Store in the refrigerator for up to 1 month.

Watercress Pesto

ITALY

LEVEL 1   YIELD: **APPROXIMATELY 2 CUPS**

Pesto is one of the classic condiments of the world. A traditional pesto with Genovese basil is a study in beautiful simplicity.

 HEART HEALTH NOTE: Watercress is in the family of Brassicaceae and helps to lower blood pressure and cholesterol levels, specifically LDL. Watercress' high polyphenol, carotenoid and chlorophyll content, as well as its strong antioxidant properties, gives watercress cancer-preventive potential and helps suppress matrix metalloproteinase-9 (MMP) activity. MMP inhibition has proven to be overall beneficial in multiple cardiovascular disease studies.

4 cups fresh watercress, washed and dried

½ cup fresh basil leaves, washed and dried

2 large ripe tomatoes

1 tablespoon freshly minced garlic

¼ cup white balsamic vinegar

¼ cup dry toasted pine nuts

1. Preheat an oven to 350°F.

2. Toast the pine nuts on a low heat in a dry pan until lightly browned and set aside.

3. Add all the ingredients to a food processor and blend on low speed until the desired consistency is reached.

4. Store in the refrigerator for up to 1 week.

Tomatillo Salsa Fresca

MEXICO

LEVEL 1   YIELD: **APPROXIMATELY 1½ CUPS**

This is a bright and versatile condiment that can be used as a garnish or sauce for just about anything—tacos, enchiladas, tamales, burgers, grilled or roasted vegetables, stews, etc.

 HEART HEALTH NOTE: Wild tomatillos can typically be found north of Mexico. The importance of wild Physalis species as a food source has been reported by many tribes as an antioxidant and have been frequently discovered in archaeological sites. These plants were cultivated by Pueblo farmers and other tribes, highlighting scratch cooking and the use of their natural tartness.

4 medium tomatillos, quartered

3 cloves garlic

1 tablespoon fresh ginger

1 cup cilantro stems and leaves, washed

1 teaspoon extra virgin olive oil

1 hot or medium chili pepper (I use serrano)

1 teaspoon Dijon mustard

1 teaspoon date syrup

2 tablespoons apple cider vinegar

1. Blend all ingredients in a food processor for a minute or the texture you prefer.

2. Store in the refrigerator for up to 1 week.

Sofrito

LATIN/SPAIN

LEVEL 1   **YIELD: APPROXIMATELY 3 CUPS**

Sofrito is a flavor starter, flavor enhancer, or finished condiment. The heart and soul of many dishes from Central and South America, and specifically, the beautiful island of Puerto Rico.

 HEART HEALTH NOTE: Vinegar has various ingredients, with the main component being 4–8 percent acetic acid. It lowers blood pressure, improves hypercholesterolemia, and suppresses body fat by acetic acid's inhibition of lipogenesis.

1 medium white onion, diced

2 cubanelle peppers, stemmed, cut into large chunks

3 ajices dulces (a sweet perennial pepper found in Latin markets, substitute yellow bell pepper)

1 small jalapeño pepper

1 teaspoon cumin powder

1 teaspoon coriander powder

¼ cup sherry or white balsamic vinegar

12 medium cloves garlic, peeled

½ large bunch cilantro, washed and roughly chopped

2 leaves of cilantro with stems

¼ bunch flat-leaf parsley

2 ripe plum tomatoes, diced

1 small red bell pepper, cored, seeded, and roughly chopped

1. In a strong food processor, blend all the ingredients until you have a smooth mixture.

2. Store in the refrigerator for up to 1 week.

Tamarind & Date Spread

INDIA

LEVEL 1　　　　　　　　　　　**YIELD: APPROXIMATELY 2½ CUPS**

This is a ubiquitous tangy, sweet, fruity, and spiced condiment found in many Indian street foods and snacks.

 HEART HEALTH NOTE: Date fruits are used as a staple food in the Middle East. They contain a good amount of dietary fiber and date fruits make for an ideal nutritional source of natural sugars. Dates have the highest concentration of polyphenols among the dried fruits and tamarind contains vitamin C which is an excellent antioxidant. Tamarind is native to Africa and other tropical regions, including India.

¼ cup tamarind paste

1 cup chopped dates

¼ cup hazelnuts

3 cups water

1 teaspoon Kashmiri red chili powder

½ teaspoon cumin powder

½ teaspoon ginger powder

1 teaspoon lemon juice

¼ cup date powder or date syrup

1. Simmer all ingredients in a heavy-bottomed saucepan on low for about 45 minutes, stirring periodically to prevent burning on the bottom.

2. When the sauce is thick enough to coat the back of a spoon, taste it and adjust the sugar and spice level.

3. Transfer everything to a blender, including the hazelnuts, and process into a smooth sauce.

4. Store in the refrigerator for up to 1 week.

Chow-Chow

SOUTHERN UNITED STATES

LEVEL 1   **YIELD: APPROXIMATELY 2 CUPS**

A distinctly Southern pickled relish that brightens any dish and one's day.

 HEART HEALTH NOTE: Bell peppers are rich sources of capsicum, carotenoids, vitamin E, and vitamin C. Peppers are associated with a lower risk of all-cause mortality and cardiovascular mortality.

1 cup cabbage, chopped

1 medium onion, chopped

1 red bell pepper, cored, chopped

1 green bell pepper, cored, chopped

1 green tomato

¼ cup sugar

½ teaspoon ground mustard

½ teaspoon ground turmeric

½ teaspoon ground ginger

½ teaspoon mustard seeds

½ teaspoon celery seed

½ teaspoon whole coriander

1 bay leaf

1 cup apple cider vinegar

1. Mix all the vegetables and let stand in a colander overnight to drain well.

2. Add the sugar and spices to the vinegar and bring to a boil and simmer for 5 minutes.

3. Add the vegetables and cook until the cabbage is soft.

4. Pack into hot jars and seal, or refrigerate after cooling. Use as desired.

Pepperonata

ITALY

This is a sweet and sour condiment made with a variety of peppers, tomatoes, fresh herbs, and bright acidity. When the vegetables are ripe and naturally sweet, the final punch of flavor is fantastically balanced. It complements any creamy flavor with the built-in vibrancy. It is also wonderful for hors d'oeuvres like crostini.

HEART HEALTH NOTE: Peppers' carotenoids are potential cardioprotective agents, while its antioxidant carotenoids work on the chronic inflammation of the arterial wall.

- 2 **medium yellow onions, sliced ¼ inch thick**
- 2 **each red, yellow, and orange bell peppers**
- 1 **teaspoon cayenne powder**
- 8 **cloves garlic, thinly sliced**
- 2 **medium ripe tomatoes**
- 2 **sprigs fresh oregano, leaves only**
- 1 **cup fresh basil leaves**
- 2 **tablespoons red wine vinegar**

1. Preheat the oven to 375°F. On a baking sheet, roast the onions, peppers, and tomatoes for about 30 minutes or until the pepper skin is blistered.

2. Peel the peppers after covering and allowing to steam.

3. In a saucepan, heat the garlic for a couple of minutes.

4. Add the roasted vegetables and the red wine vinegar and cook on a medium heat until most of the moisture has evaporated.

5. Transfer the cooked mixture, fresh herbs, and cayenne into a food processor and blend to a semi-coarse consistency.

6. Taste and adjust the seasoning as desired. Add more vinegar and spice for punch.

7. Serve at any temperature. Store in the refrigerator for up to 1 week.

Manchurian

INDIA/CHINA

LEVEL 2   **YIELD: APPROXIMATELY 2 QUARTS**

Manchuria is a region in today's north-east China. Indo-Chinese cuisine is popular throughout north-eastern India and, thanks to the melting pot that is Mumbai, an extremely popular cuisine in my hometown. There is sweet and sour, and then, there is Manchurian. Gobi (cauliflower) Manchurian is a popular appetizer in many Indian restaurants, but this sauce extends that application and is wonderful for a quick roast or as a dipping sauce. This sauce is also great on Banh Mi sandwiches and tacos.

 HEART HEALTH NOTE: Cilantro has a vasodilator effect that occurs through Ca++ channel blockade and endothelial-dependent pathways. These help to balance the management and treatment of hypertension.

1 medium red onion, diced

1 cup scallion, chopped

1 green bell pepper, cored and diced

1 jalapeño with seeds, diced

1 tablespoon ginger, minced

1 tablespoon garlic, minced

1 bunch cilantro (chop stems and leaves separately)

1 tablespoon cumin powder

1 tablespoon coriander powder

1 teaspoon turmeric powder

1 cup chopped tomatoes

½ cup light date powder

1 cup water

1. In a saucepan, heat the onions, scallions, cilantro stems, and green pepper for about 5 minutes.

2. Next, add the ginger, garlic, and jalapeno. Stir for 30 seconds.

3. Next, add the cumin, coriander, turmeric, some pepper and stir for a minute.

4. Now add the tomatoes and cook for about 5 minutes.

5. Finally add the remaining ingredients including the water and check the seasoning. Simmer for about 20 minutes uncovered on low heat. Stir periodically.

6. Let the sauce cool before blending with the fresh cilantro leaves.

7. Store the sauce in an airtight container in the refrigerator. It should keep for several weeks without spoiling.

Beet & Cardamom Chutney

INDIA

LEVEL 2   YIELD: **APPROXIMATELY 2 CUPS**

This chutney more closely resembles the types of chutneys I grew up with — a stand-out chutney, unique in flavor and application. Experiment for yourself.

 HEART HEALTH NOTE: Beets and beet greens are a remarkable vegetable rich in nitrates, boosting NOS. Beets are effective at increasing nitrate and nitrite levels surrounding the endothelium and promote vascular health. This is augmented when used raw.

½ teaspoon whole cumin seed

½-inch piece of fresh ginger, minced

2 cloves garlic, minced

1 teaspoon ground cardamom

1 cup grated yellow beets

1 cup grated red beets

2 green chilies or 1 small jalapeno pepper

2 tablespoons toasted and ground almonds

¼ cup chopped cilantro with stems

½ cup water, as needed

Juice and zest of 1 lemon

1. In a shallow pan, add the cumin seed and toast for 10 seconds.

2. Next, add the ginger and garlic and cook for a couple of minutes.

3. Now add the cardamom powder and stir for a few seconds before adding the water, half the grated beets, and chili pepper.

4. Cook for about 15 minutes before adding almonds.

5. Finish with the lemon juice, lemon zest, and chopped cilantro.

6. Re-season as desired, adjusting for spice and acidity. Transfer all ingredients to a food processor plus the other half of beets which are raw and pulse a few times. Store in the refrigerator for up to a week.

Roasted Red Pepper Coulis

FRANCE

LEVEL 1   YIELD: **APPROXIMATELY 1 CUP**

This condiment provides a contrast of color and bright flavor for dishes.

 HEART HEALTH NOTE: Parsley is an herb native to the Mediterranean region widely cultivated around the world which has culinary and medicinal purposes. People use parsley to treat arterial hypertension, hemorrhoids, nose bleeding and hyperlipidemia. Parsley inhibits blood platelet aggregation and adhesion to collagen under flow; hence its effects in preventing arterial thrombosis.

1 large red pepper
1 shallot, minced
1 teaspoon fresh ginger, minced
1 tablespoon red wine vinegar
¼ cup flat-leaf parsley
Water, as needed

1. Roast the red pepper in the oven at 350°F for about 30 minutes.

2. Place in a bowl and cover it for a few minutes, so it peels easily.

3. Roast the shallot and ginger in a pan for about 30 seconds.

4. Puree the roasted red pepper, cooked shallots, ginger, pepper, vinegar, and parsley to a smooth consistency, adding some water, as needed.

5. Adjust the seasoning as desired.

6. Store in the refrigerator for up to 1 week.

Mango Masala

INDIA

Finally, a chutney in the style of an English interpretation of Indian chutney: one with ripe fruit. I make an exception here because it would be a travesty to not showcase the queen of all fruit. The Alphonso mango is legendary in India. The Portuguese are said to have introduced grafting techniques, which allowed for varieties like the Alphonso to develop. Mango pulp (either Kesar or Alphonso) combined with many traditional chutney ingredients will harmonize into a spectacular condiment. One can control the natural sweetness of the fruit with complementary acidity and spice.

 HEART HEALTH NOTE: Mangos have different polyphenolic compounds in their pulp, peel, seed, bark, leaf, and flower. Some of the health benefits found in mangos include polyphenols, flavonoids (catechin and epicatechin), and phenolic acids (benzoic and gallic). These have protective effects against heart disease.

1 medium red onion, small dice

1 tablespoon fresh ginger, minced

1 teaspoon minced garlic

½ jalapeño, minced

1 tablespoon light date powder

2 teaspoons cumin powder

1 teaspoon coriander powder

½ teaspoon cayenne pepper

1 teaspoon turmeric powder

1 cup ripe tomatoes, diced

1 tablespoon red wine vinegar

1 can mango puree (available at most Indian grocery stores)

Water, as needed

1. In a saucepan, cook the onions and ginger over medium heat until slightly caramelized.

2. Add the garlic and jalapeno and cook for 30 seconds.

3. Next, add the date powder, cumin, coriander, cayenne, and turmeric. Cook for a minute over low-medium heat.

4. Add the tomatoes, and red wine vinegar. Cook for 2 minutes.

5. Now add the mango puree and stir well. Test to see if more acidity or pepper is needed.

6. Add water if necessary and simmer on low heat for 30 minutes, stirring frequently.

7. Let the mixture cool. Blend to the desired consistency and store in airtight containers in the refrigerator.

Spices & Seasonings

STORE BOUGHT SPICE BLENDS can be expensive, stale, and often laden with sodium and preservatives. By stocking whole spices and investing in a good coffee grinder to be used exclusively for blending spices, you will discover the incredible health benefit of spices along with the opportunity to become creative based on your own likes and preferences. In this section, you will find a variety of globally-inspired spice blends, along with notes about their geographical influence, and of course, recommended applications.

Garam Masala

INDIA

LEVEL 1   **YIELD: APPROXIMATELY ¼ CUP**

This is a general-purpose blend of spices. Some have likened it to an Indian version of French herbs de Provence or Chinese five-spice powder. The word "garam" means hot or pungent, while the word "masala" simply refers to any spice or aromatic blend. This blend is not pungent, but it is simultaneously distinctive and subjective. The fragrance and aroma can be intoxicating. Dry toast the whole spices for a few minutes on low heat before grinding in spice grinder. Note: There is no "r" in masala.

HEART HEALTH NOTE: Star anise reduces the levels of inflammatory cytokines, such as TNF-α and IL-1β, and aids in treating atherosclerotic vascular disease. Coriander seeds inhibit the production of total cholesterol and lower LDL, triglycerides, and plaque formation.

6 cardamom pods (green or white)

1 tablespoon coriander seed

2 teaspoons cumin seed

1 teaspoon black peppercorn

1 teaspoon fennel seed

1 cinnamon stick

1 dry bay leaf

1 piece star anise

1. Dry toast all the spices in a medium skillet over medium heat. Stir frequently. Toast for about 5 minutes or until you begin to sense the aroma.

2. Allow the mixture to cool a bit before transferring it to a spice grinder and process to a fine blend.

Ras El Hanout

MOROCCO

LEVEL 1   **YIELD:** APPROXIMATELY ½ CUP

Ras El Hanout is a complex, aromatic Moroccan spice blend. Most recipes include cardamom, nutmeg, anise, mace, cinnamon, ginger, various peppers, and turmeric, but 30 or more ingredients might be used. Typically prepared by grinding together whole spices, dried roots, and leaves, this recipe keeps things simple by using mostly spices. Ras El Hanout's literal translation from Arabic is "head of the shop," implying that it is "the best (or top) of the shop." Some Moroccans use it in daily cooking; others reserve it for specialty dishes. You can use Ras El Hanout to season tagines, stews, vegetables, and even ratatouille. It keeps well for several months.

 HEART HEALTH NOTE: There is a long history in Ayurvedic and traditional Chinese medicine of using turmeric for the treatment of CVD. Its key activity is as an anti-inflammatory, lipid-lowering agent, and cardioprotective element.

2 teaspoons ground ginger	**¼ teaspoon ground cloves**
2 teaspoons ground cardamom	**½ teaspoon ground anise seeds**
1 teaspoon turmeric	**2 teaspoons ground mace**
1 teaspoon smoked paprika	**1 teaspoon ground allspice**
1 teaspoon sweet paprika	**1 teaspoon ground coriander seed**
1 teaspoon cayenne or another dried chili powder	**1 teaspoon ground nutmeg**
1 teaspoon whole cumin seeds	**½ teaspoon ground black pepper**
1 teaspoon whole fennel seeds	**½ teaspoon ground white pepper**

1. Toast all the ingredients in a large dry pan on low-medium heat until you can detect the fragrance.

2. Blend all ingredients in a dedicated spice grinder until you have a smooth powder.

3. Store in an airtight container for up to 6 months.

Bahārāt

MIDDLE-EAST

LEVEL 1   YIELD: **APPROXIMATELY 1 CUP**

Not to be confused with Bharat—the Hindi (via Sanskrit) word for India. Bahārāt (the Arabic word for spices) is a delicate blend that highlights dishes native to the Middle East but is equally at home in Turkish and even Greek dishes. The assertive use of warm spices is perfect for applications that demand roasting or baking.

HEART HEALTH NOTE: Black peppercorn aids in lipid metabolism and inhibition of ROS production. Cinnamon prevents cardiovascular disease by significantly reducing the rate of dyslipidemia and platelet aggregation.

3 tablespoons black peppercorns

2 tablespoons coriander seed

1-inch piece of cinnamon stick

1 teaspoon whole clove

2 tablespoons cumin seed

4 whole green cardamom pods

1 tablespoon ground nutmeg or 1 whole nutmeg

¼ cup paprika

¼ cup sesame seeds

1. Dry toast all whole spices in a thick-bottomed pan, like a cast-iron skillet, on a low to medium flame. Stir periodically to prevent burning the spices.

2. After 10 minutes, add the remaining ingredients and toast on a slow flame for an additional 5 minutes before setting aside to cool.

3. Blend all ingredients in a dedicated spice grinder until you have a smooth powder.

4. Store in an airtight container for up to 6 months.

Jerk Seasoning

JAMAICA

LEVEL 1   **YIELD: APPROXIMATELY 1 CUP**

The term *jerk* refers to a style of cooking (marinating, roasting/smoking) as well as a blend of spices as a dry rub or a wet marinade. Best as a marinade followed by grilling or roasting. It is pungent, earthy, and full-flavored.

HEART HEALTH NOTE: Date powder is better than sugar as it is a whole food. The flavonoids in citrus improve cholesterol and lower blood pressure. Sesame or pumpkin seeds are also high in L-arginine.

1 tablespoon whole allspice

1 tablespoon whole black peppercorn

1 tablespoon whole cumin seed

1 teaspoon whole coriander seed

1 tablespoon sesame or pumpkin seeds

1 bunch scallions

4 cloves fresh garlic

1 tablespoon fresh ginger

2 Scotch Bonnet (or habanero) peppers

4 tablespoons fresh thyme

4 fresh sage leaves with stems

1 fresh orange, juice and zest

½ bunch fresh cilantro (with stems)

2 tablespoons red wine vinegar

1 teaspoon light date powder or preferably, date powder

1 medium onion

1. Toast and coarse grind the allspice, black peppercorns, cumin seeds, coriander seeds, and sesame seeds.

2. Add the ground spice mixture to the scallions, onion, garlic, ginger, peppers, thyme, sage, orange juice and zest, cilantro, vinegar, and date powder, into a food processor. Blend well. This is the jerk paste.

3. Store in the refrigerator for up to 1 month.

Chinese 5-Spice

CHINA

LEVEL 1   YIELD: **APPROXIMATELY ¼ CUP**

The blend is very fragrant, so less can be more. Good for cast-iron cooking or grilling.

 HEART HEALTH NOTE: Fennel can dissolve fat deposits in the bloodstream as an energy source, while its phenolic compounds and flavonoids (like naringin) can significantly reduce LDL and cholesterol.

2-inch piece cinnamon stick

10 whole cloves

2 teaspoons fennel seed

3 star anise

2 teaspoons Sichuan peppercorns

1. Dry toast all the spices in a heavy-bottomed pan, like a cast iron skillet, for 10 minutes on low to medium heat.

2. Blend all ingredients in a dedicated spice grinder until you have a smooth powder.

3. Store in an airtight container for up to 6 months.

Tuscan Spice Blend

ITALY

LEVEL 1   YIELD: **APPROXIMATELY ¼ CUP**

This blend is ideal for soups, stews, and roasts.

 HEART HEALTH NOTE: Plant sterols, found in herbs, spices, vegetables, nuts, seeds, cereal products, and legumes are cholesterol-lowering agents that have protective effects against cardiovascular disease.

4 teaspoon dried basil

2 teaspoons dried rosemary

3 teaspoons dried oregano

2 teaspoons garlic powder

2 teaspoons paprika

2 teaspoons ground fennel

Mix all the ingredients well and store in an airtight container.

Adobo Seasoning
LATIN/CARIBBEAN

LEVEL 1   YIELD: **APPROXIMATELY ¼ CUP**

Adobo, widely considered a national dish of sorts, is a specific style with origins in the Philippines. However, in many parts of Caribbean and Mexican cooking, the term *adobo* refers to a distinctive flavor profile obtained by the addition of a specific type of spice blend. The term *adobo* is a style of cooking, a specific dish, a sauce, and also a blend of spices.

 HEART HEALTH NOTE: Garlic improves cholesterol. Onion is an anti-inflammatory and has been shown to help fight cancers. Pumpkin seeds are antioxidants and high in L-arginine, which helps improve nitric oxide production.

1 tablespoon paprika

2 teaspoons black peppercorn

2 teaspoons onion powder

1 teaspoon dried oregano

2 teaspoons cumin seed

1 teaspoon garlic powder

1 teaspoon chili powder

1 tablespoon pumpkin seed

1. Dry toast all the ingredients for 10 minutes in a heavy-bottomed pan, like a cast iron skillet.

2. Let the mixture cool before grinding to desired fineness.

3. Store in an airtight container for up to 6 months.

Herbs de Provence

FRANCE

LEVEL 1   **YIELD: APPROXIMATELY ½ CUP**

The vineyards in Provence are stunning enough, but the lavish fields of lavender and wild rosemary capture the beauty of the region and this spice blend expresses it almost perfectly. The blend is distinctively Provencal and ideal to use during roasting or grilling.

 HEART HEALTH NOTE: Herbs de Provence are a good source of plant sterols, a cholesterol mimicker that helps reduce cholesterol intake. The American Heart Association recommends a minimum intake of 1g of plant sterols per day to show cholesterol-lowering effects.

2 tablespoons dried oregano

3 tablespoons dried thyme

2 teaspoons dried basil

½ teaspoon rubbed sage

2 tablespoons ground savory

1 tablespoon dried lavender flowers or 1 tablespoon ground lavender

Mix all the ingredients well and store in an airtight container.

Creole Seasoning

LOUISIANA

LEVEL 1   YIELD: **APPROXIMATELY 1 CUP**

Is it *Creole* or *Cajun*? A common cause of confusion, but the terms should not be used interchangeably. While there are definite commonalities, one distinction is place of origin. *Creole* is considered more a product of New Orleans, the behemoth of culture and identity in the state of Louisiana. *Creole* is the formal amalgamation of Spanish, Caribbean, and especially French influences. *Cajun*, on the other hand, is influenced by the Acadiana region of the southwestern part of the state, also with a strong French influence. Some references refer to the presence of tomatoes in *Creole* and absence/omission of tomatoes in *Cajun* cuisine. The origins notwithstanding, this blend is wonderful for sauces and in marinades prior to grilling or roasting.

 HEART HEALTH NOTE: Paprika and chili are both high in vitamin C (an anti-oxidant), which nicely complements the benefits of onion and garlic. Cumin is an anti-inflammatory and a digestive.

1 tablespoon paprika

2 teaspoons black peppercorn

2 teaspoons onion powder

1 teaspoon dried oregano

2 teaspoons cumin seed

1 teaspoon garlic powder

1 teaspoon chili powder

1. Dry toast all the ingredients for 10 minutes in a heavy-bottomed pan, like a cast iron skillet.

2. Blend all ingredients in a dedicated spice grinder until you have a smooth powder.

3. Store in an airtight container for up to 6 months.

Glossary

MEDICAL TERMINOLOGY

Antioxidant: Antioxidants are compounds that inhibit oxidation, a chemical reaction that can produce free radicals and chain reactions that may damage the cells of organisms.

Arrhythmia: A condition in which the heart beats with an irregular or abnormal pattern.

Blood Pressure: The pressure of circulating blood against the walls of blood vessels.

Cardiac Recovery: A medically supervised program or regimen designed to help improve cardiovascular health—especially after a heart attack, heart failure, angioplasty, or heart surgery.

Cardiovascular Disease (CVD): A group of diseases of the heart and blood vessels, including coronary heart disease, stroke, heart failure, heart arrhythmias, and heart valve problems.

Cholesterol: A fat-like, waxy substance that helps your body make cell membranes, many hormones, and vitamin D. The cholesterol in the blood comes from two sources: the foods a person eats and the liver.

Diabetes: A group of diseases that result in too much sugar in the blood (high blood glucose).

Fiber: A type of carbohydrate that the body cannot digest.

Free Fats: Any fat that is additional to the natural lipids contained in whole foods. So, by this definition, cooking with oil is cooking with free fat.

Glycemic Index: A value between 0 and 100 used to measure how much specific foods increase blood sugar levels.

Heart-Healthy: Conducive to a healthy heart and circulatory system.

Mindfulness: Mindfulness is the basic human ability to be fully present, aware of where we are and what we're doing, and not overly reactive or overwhelmed.

Obesity: A disorder involving excessive body fat that increases the risk of health problems.

Plaque: Deposits and buildup of fatty matter, cholesterol, calcium, and other substances within the lumen or canal of an artery or arteriole.

Sodium: An essential nutrient that is needed in small amounts by the body.

FOOD TERMINOLOGY

Agar-Agar: Vegetarian substitute for traditional gelatin, made from red sea algae; also, a binder.

Aquafaba: Leftover liquid after cooking chickpeas; whip with cream of tartar for vegan mayo.

Bhaji: Indian term used to represent vegetables; may also represent a cooked-vegetable dish without gravy.

Blistered: Result of cooking quickly on high heat, so as to brown and tear the protective skin.

Braise: Classic French cooking technique involving browning and slow-cooking in a moist medium.

Cassoulet: Hearty French stew involving proteins and white beans cooked slowly in an earthenware pot.

Chowder: Type of stew made with milk or cream thickened with a blond roux (equal parts oil and flour).

Coulis: Sauce made by puréeing vegetables or fruits; the ingredients may be cooked or uncooked.

Curry: Colonial stereotype of gravy-style dishes inspired from cuisines of the Indian subcontinent.

Dal: Ubiquitous term used in India for a preparation of legumes. Usually, dal is a purée or stew.

Demi: Sauce made by reducing approximately half the volume in order to intensify flavors.

Fra Diavolo: Spicy Italian red sauce made with or without tomato. Translates to "brother devil" in Italian.

Gazpacho: Iberian (Spain) cold soup made with raw fresh vegetables.

Grain: Small, hard seed with or without the hull; wheat, rice, corn, oats, sorghum, millet, rye, millet, etc.

Gumbo: Roux-based soup containing the "holy trinity" of onions, celery, and bell pepper. Typically, with okra.

Heirloom: Old cultivar or plant, not hybrid. Typically handed down through multiple generations.

Kofta: Meatball or meatball-style item found in many dishes from the Indian subcontinent and Middle East.

Korma: Creamy sauce typically containing gentle spices, nuts, cream and/or yoghurt.

Legume: Also known as pulse. Seed or other part of certain plants; beans, peanuts, lentils, peas, etc.

Marinade: Sauce typically made with oil, citrus, herbs, etc. Meant to infuse flavor into items before cooking.

Masarepa: A special precooked corn flour that is used to make corn cakes called *arepas*.

Masala: Typically a blend of spices. Also used in names of dishes to suggest specific combinations of spices.

Mirepoix: Flavor base made by cooking onions, carrots, and celery in butter or oil; vegetables in a 4:2:1 ratio.

Mis en Place: Everything in Place—having all the preparation ready and organized makes for a better outcome.

Momo: Steamed dumpling from the Himalayan regions of the Indian subcontinent.

Plant-Based: A plant-based diet is a diet consisting entirely of plant-based foods. Many definitions allow for the consumption of some animal products; however, in this book, we don't.

Provençal: Relating to things or people from the Provence region of France.

Pulao: Sometimes referred as pilau; a rice dish made with a flavorful broth and vegetables.

Purloo (also perloo): Regionalized rice dish from the Southern United States and parts of the Caribbean.

Seitan: Hydrated and cooked wheat gluten. Used as a vegan substitute for meat.

Socarrat: Crust formed in the bottom of the pan when cooking rice. Intentional outcome for paella.

Sofrito: Aromatic condiment common in Latin American. Also refers to beginning step of sauce-making.

Spice: Aromatic or pungent ingredient typically obtained from roots, seeds, or barks. Used to flavor food.

Sustainable: The ability to maintain levels without compromising the ability to do so in the future.

Tajine: Traditional Algerian and Moroccan dish as well the earthenware utensil in which the dish is cooked.

Tempeh: Product made from fermented soybeans—said to have originated in Indonesia.

Umami: Sense of taste referring to something being savory. Said to be one of the five senses of taste.

Wat: Stew; traditional in many North African cuisines.

Whole Food: Food that has been processed or refined as little as possible and is free from additives or other artificial substances.

Resources

HEART HEALTH FUNDAMENTALS

1. **American Heart Association**
   www.heart.org

2. **Centers for Disease Control and Prevention**
   www.cdc.gov/heartdisease

3. **Million Hearts 2027 (Centers for Disease Control and Prevention)**
   millionhearts.hhs.gov

4. **National Heart, Lung, and Blood Institute (NHLBI)**
   www.nhlbi.nih.gov

5. **U.S. Department of Agriculture**
   www.nutrition.gov/topics/diet-and-health-conditions/heart-health

6. **National Institute on Aging**
   www.nia.nih.gov/health/topics/heart-health

HEART HEALTHY DIETS & LIFESTYLE

1. **6 Lifestyle Changes Patients Should Make to Prevent Heart Disease (American Medical Association)**
   www.ama-assn.org/delivering-care/hypertension/6-lifestyle
   -changes-patients-should-make-prevent-heart-disease

2. **Keeping Your Heart Healthy (Heart Foundation)**
   www.heartfoundation.org.au/bundles/healthy-living-and-eating/
   keeping-your-heart-healthy

3. **U.S. Department of Health and Human Services**
   health.gov/myhealthfinder/health-conditions/heart-health

4. **Centers for Disease Control and Prevention**
   www.cdc.gov/heartdisease/american_heart_month_patients.htm

5. **What Is Heart-Healthy Living? (National Heart, Lung, and Blood Institute)**
   www.nhlbi.nih.gov/health/heart-healthy-living

6. **American College of Lifestyle Medicine**
   lifestylemedicine.org/patient

7. **Mayo Clinic**
   www.mayoclinic.org/diseases-conditions/heart-disease/in-depth/heart-disease-prevention/art-20046502

SLEEP & HEART HEALTH

1. **Sleep Plays an Important Role in Heart Health (The American Heart Association)**
   www.heart.org/en/health-topics/sleep-disorders/sleep-and-heart-health

2. **Centers for Disease Control and Prevention**
   www.cdc.gov/bloodpressure/sleep.htm

3. **Why You Need to Get Enough Sleep for a Healthy Heart (The Cleveland Clinic)**
   health.clevelandclinic.org/for-a-healthy-heart-get-enough-sleep

4. **How Sleep Deprivation Affects Your Heart (Sleep Foundation)**
   www.sleepfoundation.org/sleep-deprivation/how-sleep -deprivation-affects-your-heart

5. **Sleep: Important Considerations for the Prevention of Cardiovascular Disease (PubMed Central, National Library of Medicine)**
   www.ncbi.nlm.nih.gov/pmc/articles/PMC5056590

FOOD SHOPPING FOR HEART-HEALTH

1. **Heart-Healthy Foods: Shopping List (U.S. Department of Health and Human Services)**
   health.gov/myhealthfinder/health-conditions/heart-health/
   heart-healthy-foods-shopping-list

2. **Stocking a Heart-Healthy Kitchen (Cleveland Clinic)**
   my.clevelandclinic.org/health/articles/11916-stocking-a-heart
   -healthy-kitchen

3. **H. Pulapaka & J. Pulapaka, 10 Best Foods for Heart Health (Vegan Magazine)**
   www.vegan-magazine.com/2022/02/09/10-best-foods-for
   -heart-health

COOKING TIPS FOR HEART HEALTH

1. **Boosting Flavor Without Salt (American Diabetes Association)**
   www.diabetesfoodhub.org/articles/7-tips-for-creating-flavorful
   -meals-without-salt.html

2. **Building Flavor Without the Salt (Bon Appétit)**
   www.bamco.com/blog/building-flavor-without-the-salt

3. **Cooking Without Oil, Without Sacrificing the Flavor (Ornish Living)**
   www.ornish.com/zine/cooking-without-oil

4. **Menus for Heart-Healthy Eating: Cut the Fat and Salt (Mayo Clinic)**
   www.mayoclinic.org/diseases-conditions/heart-disease/in-depth/
   heart-healthy-diet/art-20046702

About the Authors

Hari Pulapaka was born and raised in Mumbai and has lived in the United States since 1987. After completing his Ph.D. in Mathematics at the University of Florida in 1995, a professional midlife crisis led to a fast-paced, top-of-the-class graduation with an Associate of Applied Science in the Culinary Arts from Le Cordon Bleu-Orlando in 2004.

Recognized by the James Beard Foundation on multiple occasions, Hari has, by invitation, frequently cooked at the historic James Beard House in New York City and was a featured chef at the 2018 James Beard Awards in Chicago. In 2016, Hari was recognized as a GRIST 50 fixer for his innovative and active work in the area of food waste reduction. Hari is a World-chefs Certified Master Chef (WCMC), a Certified Executive Chef (CEC) and an inductee into the American Academy of Chefs (AAC) of the American Culinary Federation.

When he is not teaching undergraduate Mathematics, cooking, speaking, writing about food, or running his company The Global Cooking School, Hari serves on multiple national advocacy groups for improving food systems. Hari cares deeply about thoughtful eating and a mindful existence. In addition to being a full-time chef, Hari has been a full-time and tenured Associate Professor of Mathematics at Stetson University since 2000.

Dr. Jenneffer Pulapaka's expertise in wound care and podiatric surgery has helped thousands of patients over the last 17 years. She founded her practice, DeLand Foot and Leg Center, in a community where less than 10% of the surgeons were women at the time. It is the first and longest-running female surgical practice in West Volusia County. She is the first Podiatrist to be a Board Certified Physician Diplomate in Lifestyle Medicine, "I believe every patient needs a physician who will be an advocate to help them regain their health." She became a Certified Wound Specialist Physician (CWSP) in 2016, then certified with the American Board of Multiple Specialties in Podiatry—Prevention and Treatment of Diabetic Foot Wounds and Diabetic Footwear, and Board Certified with the American Board of Wound Healing—Physician Certification in Wound Care (PCWC); holding three board certification in wound care. Additionally, she completed her Plant-Based Nutrition Certification and Culinary Health Education Fundamentals (CHEF) Coaching. She became a vegetarian in 1991 and converted to a WFPB diet in 2018.

Dr. Pulapaka and her husband are the initial two founders, now retired, of a Central Florida restaurant dedicated to improving our food system through local sources, sustainable practices, and refined flavors. "The preservation of health will not come from our Nation's leaders. It begins in our homes, in our kitchens, with our family and friends. The success and survival of our health are dependent upon knowing our vulnerabilities, and out of that knowledge will come strength, if we learn the lessons presented."

Index